AND THEN THEY PRAYED

MOMENTS IN AMERICAN HISTORY IMPACTED BY PRAYER

BARRY LOUDERMILK

God Bless!

PUBLISHED BY FASTPENCIL

Published by FastPencil
3131 Bascom Ave.
Suite 150
Campbell CA 95008 USA
info@fastpencil.com
(408) 540-7571
(408) 540-7572 (Fax)
http://www.fastpencil.com

First Edition

This book is dedicated to my Mother who, in December 2002, went home to be with our Lord, and my Father, a WWII veteran, who instilled in me a dedicated love of Jesus Christ, an appreciation for our nation's history, and good ole fashion patriotism.

༂ช

Acknowledgments

My heartfelt gratitude goes out to my family, who sacrificed much time and energy to make this book possible. I would like to especially thank my wife, Desiree, who not only put up with my countless hours of research, but endured endless nights of my reading and writing. I could never adequately express my appreciation for the hours she spent reading and editing these stories.

Special recognition is also due to our three grown children Travis, Christiana and Michael, who have assisted, through the years, listening to and reading my stories, as well as sharing ideas and editing.

CONTENTS

INTRODUCTION

In the fall of 1746, the Governor of the Massachusetts colony received an alarming message; ninety six French vessels were assembling off the coast of New England, preparing to attack Boston. With forty well armed warships and fifty six troop transports, it was the largest Naval Armada to ever approach the American colonies. Their mission was to destroy coastal cities from Massachusetts to Georgia and, aboard the warships, sailors were already preparing their cannon to lay siege on Boston. Aboard the transports, 13,000 soldiers prepared to invade and burn what remained.

The colonies had few coastal defenses and their militias were no match for the highly trained and experienced soldiers of the French Army, but Governor William Shirley had a responsibility to protect the Massachusetts colony and its' citizens. As the impending invasion was only days away, Governor Shirley needed to take quick and decisive action.

The colonists had only one reliable weapon at their disposal capable of thwarting such a massive invasion, and Governor Shirley immediately called the people to prepare for battle. He issued an official proclamation calling for citizens all across the colony to assemble in their churches for a day of fasting and prayer.

On the morning of October 16, hundreds of Bostonians made their way to the city's Old South Church where they would assemble together to pray for God's Divine intervention. The autumn morning brought a clear, calm sky, making for a pleasant walk to the church building. Once the congregation had assembled in the sanctuary, Reverend Thomas Prince ascended the high pulpit and immediately began a strong and fervent prayer. "Deliver us from our enemy," he prayed emphatically, "Send thy tempest, Lord, upon the waters to the eastward!"

Reverend Prince's powerful voice echoed off of the church's stone walls as he prayed, "Raise Thy right hand. Scatter the ships of our tormentors and drive them hence." Filled with emotion, he lifted his head toward heaven and continued to call upon God to not only protect the people from harm, but to destroy the French fleet. Suddenly, the sunlight, which only moments earlier illuminated the sanctuary, disappeared. Outside, the clear skies gave way to ominous clouds that enveloped the church in their dark shadows. At that moment, a tremendous wind slammed into the church, and the windows shook violently as they strained to hold back the tempest. The pounding of heavy rain on the church's roof reverberated inside the sanctuary. Undaunted by the raging storm outside, Reverend Prince continued his prayer, "Sink their proud frigates beneath the power of Thy winds," he cried out. He paused momentarily just as the church's bell rang twice with a strange and uneven tone. As there was no one in the bell tower, the Reverend took this to be a sign from God.

Reverend Prince raised both hands toward heaven and, with a voice of victory exclaimed, "We hear Thy voice, O Lord! We hear it! Thy breath is upon the waters to the eastward, even upon the deep. Thy bell tolls for the death of our enemies!" Silently, he lowered his hands and bowed his head before the great congregation. For several moments he stood motionless. Then, with tears streaming down his cheeks, he raised his head and, closing the prayer he proclaimed, "Thine be the glory, Lord. Amen and amen!"

Hearing of Reverend Prince's prayer and the miraculous storm that ensued, Governor Shirley sent the sloop, *The Rising Son,* northward to obtain news of the French fleet. When she returned, the captain gave an astonishing report; nearly the entire fleet had been lost in the storm. Distraught by what had befallen their mighty fleet, the French Admiral, the Duke of d'Anville and Vice Admiral d'Estournelle had taken their own lives. Of the 13,000 soldiers, only about a thousand survived, and a majority of these were severely ill and unfit for battle. The few ships still afloat were reported as being under sail, returning to France.

As He had done so many times before, God had again delivered America from the hands of their enemies. When their liberty, safety, and security were threatened, the people of Boston had prepared their homes and property for the invasion and then, they prayed.

The account of this miracle is well documented, and was once as well known as the story of Paul Revere. The American poet, Henry Wadsworth Longfellow, who penned the famous poem *Paul Revere's Ride,* also wrote of this miraculous event in the poem, *The Ballad of the French Fleet.*

One hundred and ninety seven years after Reverend Prince stood in the pulpit at Old South Church and prayed for God's deliverance, America was again in desperate need of divine assistance. On June 6, 1944 the United States and its allies were landing on the beaches of Normandy, in order to liberate France from the grip of Nazi Germany. Just as Reverend Thomas Prince had climbed to the high pulpit in Old South Church to lead the people of Boston in prayer, President Franklin Roosevelt took to the airwaves and led the people of the United States in prayer for our soldiers, sailors and airmen.

Through the crackle and static of thousands of radios across the nation, Roosevelt made his appeal to heaven. "Almighty God," he prayed, "Our sons, pride of our nation, this day have set upon a mighty endeavor, a struggle to preserve our republic, our religion, and our civilization, and to set free a suffering humanity." From New York to California, millions of Americans huddled around their radio sets, with bowed heads, as the Commander in Chief continued his solemn prayer, "Lead them straight and true; give strength to their arms, stoutness to their hearts, steadfastness in their faith."

Just as Governor Shirley called the people of Boston to fast and pray for deliverance, Roosevelt knew the nation needed God's protection in this difficult hour. He also knew that the enemy was strong and the fight would be long and arduous. "But because the road is long and the desire is great," Roosevelt implored, "I ask that our people devote themselves in a continuance of prayer. As we rise to each new day, and again when each day is spent, let words of prayer be on our lips, invoking Thy help to our efforts."

The President of the United States had assembled a congregation of men, women and children all across the nation in a united appeal to heaven. "With Thy blessing, we shall prevail over the unholy forces of our enemy. Help us to conquer the apostles of greed and racial arrogances." After nearly seven minutes of continuous prayer, President Roosevelt concluded, "Thy will be done, Almighty God. Amen." Again, America prayed and God answered.

Throughout the history of the United States of America, God has heard and honored our prayers as a nation. From the first permanent settlement established by the Pilgrims at Plymouth, to our soldiers currently fighting in battlefields around the world, Americans have regularly implored Divine assistance in our national undertakings. The extraordinary results of these prayers and their impact on the course of this nation have been well recorded throughout our history. However, these fascinating stories that were once quite commonly known among Americans have, for the most part, been forgotten. Stories that were once prominent in our school textbooks have been removed due to their references to God. As a result of this censorship, these inspiring and true events that shaped our nation have been nearly purged from our national remembrance.

Fortunately, America is experiencing a resurgence of interest in our history, as citizens across this land desire to be reunited with their true heritage.

This book tells the incredible stories of thirteen miraculous events in American history that were impacted by prayer. Over a decade of extensive research has been done to ensure the accuracy of these stories. When possible, firsthand accounts of those who witnessed these incredible events have been cited.

I pray that, as you read this book, you will not only become reunited with our providential heritage, but you will also be inspired by the character of these men and their unwavering dedication to God and Country. From the freezing forests of Valley Forge, to the deadly vacuum of space, Americans have fought when their liberty was threatened, stood firm in the face of danger, conquered a fear of the unknown, prepared for battle and then, they prayed.

Barry Loudermilk

1

A PRAYER THAT SAVED A NATION

Benjamin Franklin (1787)

"Except the LORD build the house, they labour in vain that build it: except the LORD keep the city, the watchman waketh but in vain."
Psalm 127:1

The room was crowded, the air was hot, and so were the emotions of the fifty-five men assembled in the chambers of the Philadelphia State House. It was late June, 1787 and the sweltering summer heat further stoked the fiery tempers of the delegates as they engaged in heated debate. Twelve of the thirteen states had sent some of their most respected citizens to represent their interests at this Convention to revise the Articles of Confederation. The Articles of Confederation had been the governing document of the United States since the Revolutionary War;

and, while these documents had served the needs of the states during the conflict with England, they had proven to be inadequate in governing the expanding post war nation and were in great need of revision. Rhode Island's legislature refused to participate in the Convention out of concern that the members would be too tempted to abandon the Articles and create a new government. Rhode Island's fear of this assembly "making innovations on the rights and liberties of the citizens at large," appeared to be coming true, as the Convention had, by this time, abandoned revising the Articles of Confederation and was now debating the formation of a new government; a Constitutional Republic.

The sights, sounds and smells of the old State House Chambers were all too familiar to some of the Convention's delegates, as they had assembled here many times before. Eleven years earlier, some of these same men stood in this very room when the Second Continental Congress passed a resolution declaring independence from Great Britain.

During the war for independence, except for a short time the British occupied Philadelphia, the Second Continental Congress met in the State House Chambers. Throughout this period, these men, whose primary allegiance had always been to their own colonies, were suddenly united by a common cause; freedom from tyranny. Patrick Henry, a fiery orator from the Virginia legislature and a member of the First Continental Congress, expressed this unusual unifying spirit when he declared, "I am not a Virginian but an American."

Throughout the war with England, the members of the Continental Congress regularly prayed for God's divine protection. They prayed openly as a delegation and privately as individual citizens. They knew that their only hope for victory rested in the powerful hand of God, and they were neither embarrassed nor ashamed of their reliance on His Divine power. To ensure the world and future generations understood their dependence on God's protection, they included such a statement in the Declaration of Independence. The final sentence of the Declaration expresses the unity and dedication of these brave men, "And in support of this Declaration, with a firm reliance on the protection of Divine providence, we mutually pledge to each other our lives, our fortunes and our sacred honor."

Eleven years had now passed since the Declaration of Independence was adopted and signed. These brave men, who held a *firm reliance on the protection of Divine providence,* had succeeded in their quest for liberty and won their independence, but now they faced the hardships and struggles of building an independent nation.

They needed a government that would protect and serve these thirteen independent states. However, unlike the Continental Congress who assembled here, this Convention seemed to lack the unifying spirit enjoyed during the Revolution. These men were attempting a significantly more difficult and challenging task, to solidify these independent and sovereign states into a single nation. Their goal, as they would later define, was to create a government structured unlike any the world had ever seen, a government that would be described nearly a century later by President Lincoln as a government "of the people, by the people, and for the people."

In previous Conventions, each delegation represented an independent and sovereign government working with other independent and sovereign governments toward a common goal that had equal benefit for each. Although there were debates, and an occasional argument, most Conventions had been relatively calm and productive. This time, however, the fear that one state might have more influence in the national government than another, coupled with their passion to protect the sovereignty of their individual states, ignited the delegates' emotions. Debates, which far too many times resulted in all out verbal battles between delegates, were threatening to bring a disastrous end to the Convention. In fact, part of the New York delegation, frustrated by the bitter fighting and the lack of progress, had packed up and returned home.

The eventual product of this Convention, the Constitution of the United States of America, would be such a carefully crafted, uniquely structured and significantly limited form of self government, that it would appear to some to be Divinely inspired. From the perspective of an outside observer, one would assume the handiwork of the delegates was the result of years of cooperation and coordination. In reality, the fact they even completed the Convention and emerged with any type of agreement or governing document, was a miracle in itself. The document they eventually drafted and passed was indeed miraculous, especially considering that when they first convened they had not intended to create a new government, only to revise the Articles of Confederation.

The *Constitutional* Convention, as it would come to be known, had been in session for nearly five long and mostly unproductive weeks; and, from all appearances, this would possibly be the final week. So far, little progress had been made because the delegates were deadlocked on many issues, with the most prominent being how each state should be represented in a new national government. The fighting became increasingly bitter with each session, as northern states argued that representation should be based solely on population, while the southern agricultural states argued that representation should be based on the amount of cultivated land. The representation issue also sparked arguments between small and large states. Small states demanded there be a fixed number of representatives from each state regardless of size or population. All sides were firm on their convictions and none were willing to compromise.

At the beginning of the Convention, George Washington had been unanimously elected to serve as President of the Convention, in hopes that the respect all delegates held for this *hero of the Revolution* would create a sense of unity. It was the dignity and the statesmanlike demeanor of the former General that was responsible for holding the Convention together thus far, but even Washington wondered how much more quarreling they could withstand before more delegates headed back to their home states.

Washington, through a letter writing campaign, had been one of the primary reasons this Convention had taken place. In the years following the Revolution, disputes between the states had reached a critical level, and Washington proposed convening the Congress to resolve their differences. In May of 1786, Washington expressed his feelings in a letter to John Jay, "…there are errors in our national government which call for correction; … something must be done, or the fabric will fall." Washington had fought hard for this Convention and, as much as he wanted it to succeed, he maintained his dignity and remained reserved in his position as Convention President. Washington refused to join the heated debates and, when he desired to make his opinions known, he would do so privately outside the Convention chambers.

On June 28, the Convention took a catastrophic turn. Once again, the debates regarding representation ignited a fiery diatribe, which resulted in one of the small states threatening to leave the Confederation and align itself with a foreign power. A delegate from one of the larger states immediately responded with the threat of using military force to keep dissenting states in line. It was now inevitable; everything our soldiers had fought and died for was crumbling down around them. Washington had commanded many of these brave patriots through eight brutal years of war. Countless numbers of America's countrymen had given their lives for this new nation, and now, the very Convention that was supposed to design a new and stronger nation was, in reality, destroying it. To many of those in attendance, it seemed only a miracle could save the union now and, unknowingly, a miracle was about to begin.

AN APPEAL TO HEAVEN

George Washington was a man who was no stranger to miracles. During his service as the Commander of the Continental Army, he had witnessed numerous accounts of unexplainable providence in his favor. Washington believed, as he documented in many letters and journals, that God had his hand on our cause and these incidents were acts of God's divine intervention. Now Washington was in need of a new miracle; one that would change the current course of the Convention. Without such a change, it seemed impossible that they would progress any further and that all they had fought for during the war with Great Britain may have been in vain.

Another highly respected statesman, the President of Pennsylvania, was also looking for a miracle that day. The eighty-one year old Benjamin Franklin, who, like Washington, had also withheld comment through the entire Convention, sensed that the hostility had brought them to a breaking point. He knew something must be done to save the Convention, and he decided it was time to intervene. Gaining the attention of Washington, he slowly stood to speak. As he rose, the room fell deathly quiet as the prominence of the elderly statesman captured the attention of everyone. His features were old, but his voice was strong and commanding, and his words reverberated throughout the chamber. Leaning on his cane, Benjamin Franklin addressed the members of the Convention.

"*Mr. President,*" Franklin began, as he directed his opening statement to George Washington,

The small progress we have made after four or five weeks close attendance and continual reasoning with each other, our different sentiments on almost every question, several of the last producing as many noes as ays, is methinks a melancholy proof of the imperfection of the Human Understanding. We indeed seem to feel our own want of political wisdom, since we have been running about in search of it. We have gone back to ancient history for models of Government, and examined the different forms of those Republics which having been formed with the seeds of their own dissolution now no longer exist. And we have viewed Modern States all round Europe, but find none of their Constitutions suitable to our circumstances.

In this situation of this Assembly, groping as it were in the dark to find political truth, and scarce able to distinguish it when presented to us, how has it happened, Sir, that we have not hitherto once

thought of humbly applying to the Father of lights to illuminate our understanding?

In the beginning of the Contest with Great Britain, when we were sensible of danger we had daily prayer in this room for the divine protection. "Our prayers, Sir, were heard, and they were graciously answered. All of us who were engaged in the struggle must have observed frequent instances of a Superintending providence in our favor.

To that kind providence we owe this happy opportunity of consulting in peace on the means of establishing our future national felicity. And have we now forgotten that powerful Friend? or do we imagine we no longer need His assistance?

I have lived, Sir, a long time, and the longer I live, the more convincing proofs I see of this truth, that God Governs in the affairs of men. And if a sparrow cannot fall to the ground without His notice, is it probable that an empire can rise without His aid?

We have been assured, Sir, in the Sacred Writings, that "except the Lord build the House they labor in vain that build it." I firmly believe this; and I also believe that without his concurring aid we shall succeed in this political building no better than the Builders of Babel: We shall be divided by our partial local interests; our projects will be confounded, and we ourselves shall become a reproach and bye word down to future ages.

And what is worse, mankind may hereafter from this unfortunate instance, despair of establishing Governments by human wisdom and leave it to chance, war and conquest.

I therefore beg leave to move that henceforth prayers imploring the assistance of Heaven, and its blessing on our deliberations, be held in this Assembly every morning before we proceed to business, *and that one or more of the clergy of the city be requested to officiate in that service.*

Franklin completed his remarks and returned to his seat. For some time, the room remained quiet as everyone was moved with emotion. Franklin had openly rebuked the entire Convention for their failure to corporately ask God for His guidance. Virtually every one of the delegates were active members of Christian churches and, though some had sought private devotions, none had proposed praying together as a Convention. Jonathon Dayton, a delegate from New Jersey, in reporting the reaction of the delegates to Franklin's remarks stated, "The doctor sat down; and never did I behold a countenance at once so dignified and delighted as was that of Washington at the close of the address; nor were the members of the Convention generally less affected. The words of the venerable Franklin fell upon our ears with a weight and authority."

Mr. Roger Sherman, a delegate from Connecticut, moved by Franklin's admonition, promptly seconded his motion. A discussion ensued, as some of the delegates wanted to debate the matter. Those delegates were not opposed to Franklin's suggestion but, as Alexander Hamilton expressed, this was something they should have done at the beginning of the Convention instead of waiting until now. He argued that if they suddenly bring a member of the clergy into their daily deliberations, the public might get the idea that dissentions within the Convention had called for such measures. Franklin, Sherman and others argued that the past omission of such a duty could not justify a further omission. Mr. Hugh Williamson of North Carolina brought to everyone's attention that the true reason that the clergy had not been included is that the Convention had no funds to pay a chaplain.

Mr. Edmond Randolph of Virginia offered a proposal. He suggested that a sermon be preached, at the request of the delegates, on July 4, the anniversary of independence, and henceforth prayers be offered at the beginning of each day of the Convention. Benjamin Franklin seconded the motion.

A few days later, on July 4, 1787 in response to Franklin's appeal and Randolph's proposal, the majority of the members of the Constitutional Convention, led by George Washington, assembled at the Reformed Calvinistic Church in Philadelphia. Reverend William Rogers preached a sermon about trusting the wisdom of God to establish a "free and vigorous government." Rogers's sermon filled the attendees with a new hope as he delivered these words:

We fervently recommend to the fatherly notice… Our federal convention… Favor them, from day to day, with thy inspiring presence; be their wisdom and strength; enable them to devise such measures as may prove happy instruments in healing all divisions and prove the good of the great whole… That the United States of America may form one example of a free and virtuous government…

May we… continue, under the influence of republican virtue, to partake of all the blessings of cultivated and Christian society.

When the Convention reconvened the following week, there was a new attitude among the delegates. Franklin's call for prayer had broken the deadlock that threatened to end the Convention, and a new air of cooperation had replaced the spirit of dissention. Jonathon Dayton recorded in his journal that, "Every unfriendly feeling had been expelled, and a spirit of conciliation had been cultivated."

The Constitutional Convention went back to work; but this time, the debates were civil and their differences were easily worked out through negotiations. On September 17, 1787 the final vote was called, and the Constitution of the United States of America was formally adopted. This document, beginning with the words, "We the People," not only shaped a new nation, but ultimately changed the course of history for the entire world, because of one man's call for prayer and the miracle of cooperation that resulted.

The Constitution was not the only product that resulted from Franklin's call for prayer. When the first *Constitutional Congress* of the United States convened on April 9, 1789, one of the first actions of Congress was to formally enact Benjamin Franklin's recommendation made at the Constitutional Convention. Congress formally appointed two chaplains, one to the House and one to the Senate, and each was paid a salary from the national treasury. This tradition has continued as, still today, every session of Congress is opened in prayer.

REFERENCES

Federer, William J. *America's God and Country: Encyclo-pedia of Quotations.* Coppell, TX: Fame, 1994. Print.

Flexner, James Thomas. *George Washington: the Forge of Experience, 1732-1775.* Boston: Little, Brown, 1965. Print.

Madison, James. *Notes of Debates in the Federal Convention of 1787 Reported by James Madison.* New York: Norton, 1987. Print.

M'Guire, E. C. *The Religious Opinions and Character of Washington.* New York: Harper, 1836. Print.

Morris, B. F. *Christian Life and Character of the Civil Institu-tions of the United States, Developed in the Official and Historical Annals of the Republic.* Philadelphia: G.W. Childs, 1864. Print.

U. S. —Constitutional Convention. *Debates in the Federal Convention of 1787 Which Framed the Constitution of the United States of America.* Oxford Univ. Pr., 1920. Print.

2

THE PRAYER AT VALLEY FORGE

General George Washington (1777)

"And I will bring the third part through the fire, And will refine them as silver is refined, And will try them as gold is tried: They shall call on my name, and I will hear them: I will say, It is my people:"
Zechariah 13:9

The winter of 1777 was perhaps the harshest and coldest winter the eleven thousand soldiers serving under George Washington had ever experienced. Following a devastating defeat, encountered while attempting to stop the British from taking America's prize city of Philadelphia, General George Washington needed a place to make winter camp. Scouts were sent to search the countryside near Philadelphia for a suitable location. Finally, in December, the scouts returned to inform Washington of an acceptable site only eighteen miles northwest of Philadelphia, a forested area between Valley Creek and the Schuylkill River. In a strategic sense, the site was easily defendable and the forests would provide fuel for heat and wood for shelter; however, it would not provide their most needed resource; food. Even though there were a few farms in the area, the wheat and barley fields had either been burned by the British to keep them out of the hands of the Continental Army, or stripped clean by British patrols.

On December 19, Washington mounted his horse and led his army through a bitterly cold ice storm, to their new winter dwelling at Valley Forge. As they walked, Washington saw that very few of his soldiers had shoes that totally covered their feet, some only wore rags wrapped around their feet, and others marched barefoot through the snow and ice. Washington sorrowfully watched as his men fought the frigid temperatures and driving wind to keep moving. Ice and snow pelted their nearly naked bodies; but, as Washington noted, through all their suffering, they never murmured a complaint about their conditions. Washington, in describing their condition, stated, "No history…can furnish an instance of an army's suffering such uncommon hardships as ours has done, and bearing them with the same patience and fortitude. To see men without clothes to cover their nakedness, without blankets to lie on, without shoes (for the want of which their marches might be traced by the blood from their feet)."

Initially, all eleven thousand men were forced to lived in tents; but very soon after their arrival at Valley Forge, Washington ordered all able bodied men to begin constructing cabins. These cabins, which Washington had designed himself, measured fourteen feet by sixteen feet and each would house twelve men. Since the Continental Army was comprised of many farmers, trappers and experienced woodsmen, they were able to devise structures that could be built without nails, which was important since nails were a luxury the Continental Army could not acquire. Amazingly, within a month, the Army had constructed over seven hundred of these small shelters. Now they would have some protection from the heavy snow fall and, with a crude fireplace in each dwelling, they would have a little warmth.

Washington's staff had selected a nearby farm, the home of a Quaker named Isaac Potts, to serve as the General's headquarters. However, against the wishes of his physician and staff officers, Washington remained in his leaky cold tent, refusing to move into the house until every last soldier had access to warm quarters. His staff tried to convince him that, should he become ill or die from influenza or one of the many other illnesses that were prevalent in the camp, the fight for independence would surely die with him. But Washington insisted that his own conditions would not improve until those of his men improved. Finally, to the relief of his officers and aides, the last cabin was completed and the General moved into the Potts' home.

Conditions at Valley Forge were desperate. Rations were low and meals consisted of barely enough nutrition to keep a healthy man alive. Disease and illness were rampant throughout the camp. Influenza, small pox, typhus, starvation, and exposure to the extreme winter conditions, were taking the lives of about twelve men per day. The camp was a despairing and deadly place, but Washington refused to be isolated from his Army. Early each morning, the General would mount his horse and make his rounds among the camp. Washington's visits were not to inspect the neatness of the barracks or to file his men into ranks for lengthy speeches on their duties. The General was visiting and encouraging his men out of pure compassion. Washington's physician, Doctor Thacher, said, "...his Excellency the Commander in Chief...manifested a fatherly concern and fellow-feeling for their sufferings and made every exertion in his power to remedy the evil and to administer the much desired relief."

In February, conditions worsened as the camp was down to its last twenty-five barrels of flour, and the winter weather conditions went from bad to extreme. Around this time a Congressional Committee, sent to inspect the condition of the Army, arrived. Their report to Congress of "feet and legs froze till they became black, and it was often necessary to amputate them," told a chilling but true story of life at Valley Forge. But through all their suffering, as Washington so often commented, his men never really complained. Washington reported that men would wander around the camp with such torn rags for clothes that they covered very little of their bodies, but there was little he could do other than grieve for his men. Washington wrote, "I am...convinced beyond a doubt that unless some great and capital change suddenly takes place...this Army must inevitably be reduced to one or other of these three things: starve, dissolve, or disperse..."

Washington realized that without an immediate and drastic change, the dream of independence would die with his Army at Valley Forge. The compassionate General Washington saw his men suffering and dying, and he must have also envisioned the widowed brides and orphaned children that would inevitably result from this war. As history has so often shown, there is no question that he was willing to sacrifice his own life for "the cause," but what about his men? Would he be able to lead his men into future battles knowing that some, after surviving the suffering of Valley Forge, would inevitably die on the battle-field? After all, he was fighting against the mightiest Army on the face of the Earth with what many called a "rag-tag rabble."

Since the first shots were fired at Lexington and Concord, this "rag-tag" Army had been outnumbered, out-supplied, out-gunned, and out soldiered by the British. Washington knew that he, his men, and his country were in a most desperate situation. He also knew that the decisions he would have to make very soon would determine whether the war for independence could continue.

Men of lesser countenance would have folded under such conditions; but men of strong character and moral principle, such as Washington, believe in cause, not circumstance. Washington's noble cause was freedom and he was dedicated to the fight for liberty. He believed that God, through acts of Divine providence, had often times intervened on behalf of himself and the Continental Army. Strange events that favored the Continental Army had been witnessed and recorded by both British and Americans. Storms that seemingly appeared from nowhere, stopping enemy attacks, and strange fogs that blinded the British, allowing the Americans to escape entrapments, were just some of the miraculous events that had already taken place. Washington truly believed that God was lending aid to their cause, and he often prayed for God's Divine protection and guidance.

Washington preferred to pray alone in the solitude of the forests, and he was often seen riding out into the wooded areas of

Valley Forge for private devotions. It was on one such occasion that Isaac Potts, the Quaker in whose home Washington made his headquarters, encountered Washington one evening during his prayers. Mr. Potts was returning home through the forest when he heard a voice at a distance. Struck by curiosity, Potts decided to investigate. As he drew closer, the voice became more prominent, and it had a serious and seeking tone to it. Isaac Potts approached the voice rather quietly, as not to disturb the source. Upon further inspection, he saw the figure of a man whose features he immediately recognized as the Commander in Chief of the Continental Army. Potts observed General Washington "knelt on the cold ground in prayer," and as he later expressed, Washington "was interceding for his men, his cause, and his beloved country."

Potts, a pacifist, held the belief that a soldier could not also be a Christian; therefore, he was quite amazed at the scene before him. He remained quietly hidden until the General had finished his devotions and retired. Potts, returning to his home, threw himself into a chair beside of his wife. "Heigh! Isaac!" said his wife tenderly, "thee seems agitated; what's the matter?" "Indeed, my dear," he answered, "if I appear agitated 'tis no more than what I am. I have seen this day what I shall never forget. Till now I have thought that a Christian and a soldier were characters incompatible; but if George Washington be not a man of God, I am mistaken, and still more shall I be disappointed if God does not through him perform some great thing for this country. I heard him pray, Hannah, out in the woods today, and the Lord will surely hear his prayer. He will, Hannah; thee may rest assured He will."

God indeed answered Washington's prayers, and through Washington's inspired leadership, changes that would alter the course of the war, and inevitably the entire world, began to occur.

Washington realized that the most immediate danger his Army faced was their depleted morale. He believed that this was as detrimental to the survival of his men as the sickness, starvation, and weather conditions. Again, Washington responded caringly to the needs of his men by calling for Christian church services to be held in the camp. In his order to the chaplains to establish services, Washington stated, "To the distinguished character of a patriot, it should be our highest glory to add the more distinguished character of a Christian." One of the ministers of a nearby church commented on his observance of Washington's attempt to improve the men's spirits, by stating, "His Excellency General Washington rode around among his Army yesterday and admonished each and every one to fear God, to put away the wickedness that has set in and become so general, and to practice the Christian virtues." The men responded to his call, and soon the spiritual and emotional condition of the camp began to improve.

This sudden change in morale had an effect on every aspect of life in Valley Forge. A miraculous transition occurred which some historians have termed, "the other Valley Forge." Although there was still little food, in fact some men were near starvation at this point and sickness and disease were still rampant, men's attitudes took a positive turn. Men began to laugh at their own misfortunes and joke about their nakedness. On one occasion, a group of young officers hosted a dinner to which no one with a whole pair of breeches (pants) was admitted. Slowly, by facing their desperate condition together, the Continental Army was being forged into solid hardened force. Men were forming bonds of loyalty with one another, and a sense of deep dedication to their General, who had suffered with them.

History now shows that the suffering at Valley Forge was, in reality, another act of providence. While the Americans were building their physical strength by building cabins and fighting off sickness and disease, the British were busy entertaining at social gatherings. While the Americans were foraging the forests for food, the British were attending banquets and balls. While young American patriots, with barely enough clothing to cover their bodies, were drawing water from a frozen river, the British were drinking fine wine and conversing around fireplaces. And while the Americans were attending church services in the damp cold, and praying for God to intervene on their behalf, the British were celebrating their victories over Washington and his rag-tag Army.

Historians point to Valley Forge as the turning point for the Americans in the Revolutionary War. It was through this trying time that that the American Army was forged by these harsh conditions into a formidable fighting force. They were now stronger, wiser and more dedicated to the cause of liberty. Washington wrote that, "These are the times that try men's souls. The summer soldier and the sunshine patriot will, in this crisis, shrink from the service of their country; but he that stands it now, deserves the love and thanks of man and woman."

The Continental Army, as history would record, became unstoppable in the remaining years of the Revolutionary War. Although they were greatly outnumbered, and continued to lose many more battles than they would win, the resolve they gained from that terrible winter would not allow them to give up, nor give in. Quite simply, the Continental Army would eventually win this war through perseverance. General Green explained the new American strategy this way, "We fight, get beat, rise and fight again." On virtually every front, the British became frustrated by this Army that could not be defeated.

God's providence would intervene again and again before the British would finally surrender and sail back to England. Washington would pray many more prayers for his men, his cause, and his beloved country. But because of his prayers at Valley Forge, the situation, which could have ended our war for independence, actually became the beginning of the end for the British Army.

REFERENCES

Flexner, James Thomas. *"George Washington in the American Revolution: (1775-1783)."* Boston (Mass.): Little Brown, 1968. Print.

Kelly, C. Brian., and Ingrid Smyer-Kelly. *Best Little Stories from the American Revolution.* Nashville, TN: Cumberland House, 1999. Print.

Marshall, Peter, and David Manuel. *From Sea to Shining Sea.* Old Tappan, NJ: F.H. Revell, 1986. Print.

Marshall, Peter, and David Manuel. *The Light and the Glory.* Old Tappan, NJ: Revell, 1977. Print.

Stiles, T. J. *The American Revolution: First Person Accounts by Men Who Shaped Our Nation.* New York: Berkley Pub. Group, 1999. Print.

3

PROVIDENCE SPRING

Private William Tannahill (1864)

"When the poor and needy seek water, and there is none, And their tongue faileth for thirst, I the LORD will hear them, I the God of Israel will not forsake them. I will open rivers in high places, and fountains in the midst of the valleys: I will make the wilderness a pool of water, and the dry land springs of water."
Proverbs 3:20(NLT)

"The prisoner's cry of thirst rang up heaven, God heard and with his thunder, cleft the earth and poured out his sweetest waters here." These words, etched on a stone monument, tell the story of one of the greatest acts of God's Divine intervention in America's history. It was a miracle witnessed by hundreds, recorded in the journals of dozens, and ultimately saving the lives of thousands; but, other than this lone marble structure testifying to this miracle that took place in August of 1864, little recognition is given to it by modern historians or the National Park Service. American history revisionists, the government, and even the movie industry have chosen to ignore it rather than try to explain an event that can only be defined as an act of God's hand. If it was not for a monument erected over a century ago, it is quite possible this story would be forgotten.

Today, the site of the largest and most deadly of all Civil War prison camps, Andersonville, is a solemn peaceful park with low rolling hills and serene beauty. Where Union prisoners once hastily assembled shelters called "shebangs," there is now a lush meadow where deer graze in the evenings and squirrels search the grass for fallen pecans. The place where many prisoners of war, dying of starvation, thirst and disease, spent the last miserable moments of their lives, is today a National historic park where marble and granite monuments dot the beautiful landscape. The areas where prisoners secretly dug wells in search of water and constructed tunnels to escape the torturous conditions, are now mere indentions in the earth surrounded by wrought-iron fences and historical markers. The prison ground, once encompassed by stockade walls, is now surrounded by a paved roadway where visitors can view the site without leaving the comfort of their air conditioned vehicles. Other than a small replica of the stockade wall that surrounded the twenty-six acre prison camp, little evidence of the horrors and suffering of Andersonville remains today.

The surreal beauty of this historic park challenges the mind of the visitor to imagine that this peaceful landscape was once the site of horrible deprivation, disease, and death. Just north of the prison site is the Andersonville National Cemetery where neatly aligned stone monuments mark the graves of the nearly 13,000 men who succumbed to the deplorable conditions of Andersonville. Separated from the other graves stand six small stone markers. These are the graves of the infamous Raiders, whose rampant theft, violence and murder caused additional suffering among their fellow soldiers in the camp. Signs erected around the park prohibiting recreational activities remind visitors that this is a sacred and honored place. Those who visit Andersonville expecting to see a reconstructed prison camp with high pine log stockade walls surrounding a mud soaked prison ground and artifacts from the Civil War, will leave disappointed. Time has replaced the horrors of war with the peace and beauty of nature, but to those who were imprisoned here in 1864, Andersonville was a literal hell on Earth.

In late 1863, Confederate officials determined that, with Union forces moving closer to Richmond, the Confederacy's primary prison camps should be moved southward to more secure areas. A site in Sumter County, Georgia, ten miles north of Americus was chosen. The new Confederate Prison Camp at Andersonville, conveniently located along the Southwestern Railroad, would provide a milder winter climate, a more abundant food supply, and generally better conditions for the Union soldiers who would be imprisoned there. Work began on Camp Sumter in January, 1864 and the first prisoners arrived in February. The twenty-six acre prison ground, which was no more than an open, muddy field, was surrounded by fifteen foot stockade walls of hewn pine logs. At thirty-yard intervals sentry boxes or "pigeon roosts" as the prisoners called them, were erected on top of the walls where armed Confederate guards stood watch twenty-four hours a day. To further discourage prisoners from attempting escape, a line of posts were erected about nineteen feet inside the stockade walls, marking an inner perimeter area that prisoners were forbidden to enter. This prohibited area was known as the "deadline," and the prisoners knew that anyone who crossed this line was immediately shot by the guards.

Andersonville was originally constructed to hold about 10,000 Union prisoners; however, with over four hundred prisoners arriving daily, by August of 1864 the camp held more than 33,000 prisoners. By this time, Andersonville faced more than just overcrowded conditions. The need to supply the Confederate soldiers fighting on the front lines, and the interruption of transportation in the south by advancing Union forces, caused a critical shortage of food, clothing, and other supplies. Captain Henry Wirtz, the Camp Commander, was faced with the impossible task of managing an overcrowded prison with inadequate food and supplies. Whether it was simply the result of circumstances beyond his control, or deliberate actions, Captain Wirtz would eventually be tried and executed for his mismanagement of the prison camp and the mistreatment of the Union Soldiers at Andersonville.

Living conditions at Camp Sumter were less than ideal. There were no barracks or bunkhouses constructed inside the stockade. Prisoners were forced to construct their own shelters from materials brought into the camp with them, or obtained from Confederate guards. As the prison population grew, the entire camp from wall to wall was filled with canvas tents and crudely constructed structures called "shebangs" where the prisoners, who were lucky enough to have them, could find some shelter from the searing heat and the torrential rain falls common to south Georgia. Food rations, given once a day, consisted of barely enough nourishment to keep a man alive, and often the food was spoiled, rotten or infested with insects or worms. In describing the condition of prisoners at Andersonville, Sergeant David Kennedy, a prisoner from the 9th Ohio Cavalry wrote in his personal diary, "Would that I was an artist and had the material to paint this camp and all its horrors, or the tongue of some eloquent statesman and had the privilege of expressing my mind to our honorable rulers at Washington, I should glory to describe this hell on Earth where it takes seven of its occupants to make a shadow."

Although malnutrition, sickness and exposure attributed to many deaths, the lack of clean water was the cause of most. A slow moving stream that flowed through the middle of the prison, Stockade Creek, was the only source of water for the entire prison population. This creek, which was actually nothing more than a stagnant marsh, was intended to be the prisoner's sole source of drinking water, but it was also commonly used for laundry, bathing, and as the prison's only latrine. With over 33,000 men using Stockade Creek as a latrine, the water became a breeding ground for many deadly diseases, and was so contaminated by human waste, it emitted a terrible odor. In fact, the residents in Americus, ten miles away, complained of the nauseating stench.

Drinking the water from Stockade Creek would ensure a prisoner an early transfer, from the prison to the cemetery. Nearly ninety-five percent of all deaths were caused by diarrhea and dysentery contracted by prisoners drinking from or washing in the water of Stockade Creek.

The death rate at Andersonville was astounding. By August of 1864 more than one hundred prisoners were dying each day.

The need for fresh water was critical, and many prisoners turned their efforts away from digging escape tunnels to digging fresh water wells. Although some succeeded in finding very small quantities of water, their wells quickly dried up. Some prisoners, so desperate for water, would break down and drink from Stockade Creek. Those that did were soon carried to the prison hospital or the dead-house to await burial. Others, so crazed by their thirst, purposely walked into the deadline, where they were shot to death by prison guards. For these soldiers, death was better than life inside the walls of Andersonville.

In early August, a young private of the Seventh Iowa Regiment, William Tannahill, witnessed a fellow prisoner purposely walk into the deadline, where he was immediately shot and killed by prison guards. The sight of comrades being driven to commit suicide made Private Tannahill desperate to find relief for the prisoners' thirst. Tannahill, a Christian man, along with a few others, immediately organized prayer meetings, where they purposed to specifically pray for God to send water. Josiah Young, another soldier from Iowa, joined Tannahill's prayer group and on August 9, William Tannahill, Josiah Young and several other prisoners began praying for God to send relief for the thirsty and dying men at Andersonville.

The men gathered in an area known as "the Tabernacle," which was nothing more than a hole in the ground created from the roots of a tree that had been blown down during a storm. Within about an hour after beginning their fervent prayers, the sound of thunder was heard in the distance. As the men continued their appeal to heaven, the wind began to howl through the nearby pine trees, as a tremendous thunderstorm moved in over the camp.

The sky rapidly darkened as the storm clouds began pouring down rain in torrents. Prisoners, unmindful of the wind and driving rain, began setting out pots, cups, dishes, hats, anything to catch the rainwater. This rain, as with many previous storms, would provide some temporary relief; but as soon as the storm passed, the sun would quickly evaporate most of the precious rainwater.

The rain continued to come down so heavily that part of the camp around Stockade Creek began to flood. The flood waters soon turned the stagnant swamp into a swirling current, washing the disease infested water downstream and out of the stockade.

The unexpected rainstorm was indeed cleaning the camp, but William Tannahill and his prayer group were praying for a source of fresh water, so they continued to pray. Suddenly, a tremendous clap of thunder erupted and a bright bolt of lightning burst from the sky and struck the ground just inside the stockade wall. It was then that hundreds of prisoners witnessed a miraculous sight. At the very spot where the lightning struck, a spring of clear water began bubbling up from the ground. John L. Maile of the 8th Michigan Infantry, described it as "a spring of purest crystal water shot up into the air in a column and falling in a fan like spray went babbling down the grade...Looking across the deadline we beheld with wondering eyes and grateful hearts the fountain spring."

Although the spot where the lightning struck and the spring erupted was inside the deadline, Confederate guards allowed prisoners to construct a wooden trough to carry the water into the prison grounds. The spring, which they appropriately named Providence Spring, provided enough fresh water to supply the needs of the entire camp. It can only be imagined the number of lives that were saved by the astonishing emergence of the pure water spring; yet, not only lives, but many men's souls were also saved as they witnessed the miracle of Providence Spring. The incident so affected one young prisoner from Decatur County, Tennessee, that he dedicated his life to preaching, and continued his ministry for fifty years.

With money raised by former prisoners, a marker was purchased in 1901 and placed at the site where Providence Spring had suddenly appeared. Though Andersonville is now void of stockade walls, deadlines, stagnant marshes, death-houses, shebangs and other reminders of the miseries encountered there, about halfway across the grassy field stands a lone stone monument marking the only remaining original artifact of the camp; the monument marks Providence Spring, the answer to men's prayers, which still flows today.

REFERENCES

Davis, Robert Scott. *Andersonville Civil War Prison*. Charleston, SC: History, 2010. Print.

Goss, Warren Lee. *The Soldier's Story of His Captivity at Andersonville, Belle Island, and Other Rebel Prisons*. Scituate, MA: Digital Scanning, 2001. Print.

Maile, John L. *Prison Life in Andersonville with Special Reference to the Opening of Providence Spring*. Los Angeles: Grafton Pub., 1912. Print.

McElroy, John. *Andersonville: a Story of Rebel Military Prisons* ... Toledo: Locke, 1870. Print.

Stearns, Amos E. *Narrative of Amos E. Stearns ... a Prisoner at Andersonville;*. Worcester, MA: Franklin P. Rice, 1888. Print.

Texas State Genealogical Society. Stirpes, Volume 34, Number 1, March 1994, Frances Condra Pryor, editor, Journal/ Magazine/Newsletter, March 1994; digital images,

Styple, William B. *Andersonville: Giving up the Ghost*. Kearny, NJ: Belle Grove Pub., 1996. Print.

4

TAILWINDS OF PROVIDENCE

Lieutenant Colonel "Jimmy" Doolittle (1942)

"But those who wait on the Lord Shall renew their strength; They shall mount up with wings like eagles, They shall run and not be weary, They shall walk and not faint."
Isaiah 40:31 (NKJV)

Studying maps of the Japanese mainland had suddenly replaced the nightly poker games as the primary off duty activity below the decks of the aircraft carrier, *USS Hornet*, at least for the forty-eight Army Air Corps pilots and navigators, who were the guests of the United States Navy on this highly secretive mission. The additional thirty-two Army Air Corps enlisted men who served as bombardiers, gunners and mechanics, were scouring over every detail of their Mitchell B-25 bombers strapped to the deck of the ship. Sergeant Joseph W. Manske, the mechanic and gunner of aircraft number five, meticulously checked every component of both engines to ensure his aircraft was mission ready.

It was April 17, 1942, and for two and a half months the men of the sixteen aircrews had been rigorously training for a mission so secretive that, until a few days earlier, they had not even been told their objective.

MISSION READY

Since the beginning of February, when each man had volunteered for what they were told was an extremely dangerous, but highly valuable, mission they had been experimenting and training to do things with the B-25 that it was not designed to do.

While the pilots and co-pilots were learning how to get the planes airborne in about a third the amount of runway the aircraft normally used, the mechanics were directed to make unusual modifications to the airframe and engines. Radios, and even some of the armament, were removed. Any component deemed not absolutely necessary for the plane to take off, fly and drop a few bombs, was removed to decrease weight. Carburetors, which were designed for optimal speed and performance, were recalibrated for greater fuel efficiency.

Special rubber fuel tanks were delivered, which would be placed in the crawlspace that connected the cockpit to the rear gunner's compartment, where gunners and mechanics, such as Joe Manske, sat. This would not only cut off access between the gunner and the rest of the crew, but it would render the bottom gun turret unusable, so those were also removed to lessen the weight and hopefully extend the plane's fuel range.

Each of the sixteen aircrews consisted of five men who had volunteered for this mission. Because the mission was extremely dangerous, and possibly even suicidal, the men had been given multiple opportunities to back out honorably. But none stepped aside, and they all confidently stood with their Mission Commander, Lieutenant Colonel James Doolittle.

While none of the sixteen aircrews knew exactly what they were training for, they could easily determine that it was going to be a long trip. They also correctly derived they would likely start the mission from the deck of an aircraft carrier, and that fuel range was a significant concern. But orders were precise and clear; they were not to discuss their training with anyone, including family and friends, no matter how much they were trusted. The crews were even prohibited from speculating amongst themselves where they may be going and what their target was to be. However, since the United States was now officially involved in the war in Europe and Japan, they knew they could be going just about anywhere.

A BOLD PLAN

Five months earlier, the United States had suffered the worst defeat on U.S. soil since the war of 1812. On the morning of December 7, 1941 the Japanese Navy had launched a surprise and devastating air attack on the U.S. Pacific Fleet based at Pearl Harbor, Hawaii, that had crippled America's military might in the Pacific. The attack resulted in the sinking or serious damage of eighteen ships, and the loss of almost three hundred fifty American aircraft. But the most devastating loss to the United States, was the 2,403 Americans killed and 1,178 wounded.

With the U.S. Pacific Fleet virtually out of commission, our military forces throughout the Pacific were now lacking their primary means of resupply. Our Pacific military bases, now vulnerable without the protection of naval air support, were little more than a hindrance to the Japanese, as they easily swept across the Pacific taking Guam, the Philippines and Wake Island. On February 22, President Franklin Roosevelt ordered General Douglas MacArthur to leave the Philippines and go to Australia, where he would take command of Allied troops, once they were deployed. Meanwhile, the Japanese continued their sweep across the Pacific, taking Hong Kong, Singapore, Burma, Sumatra, Java and the East Indies.

With airbases established across the Pacific, the Japanese began to focus on establishing a link to join the German forces battling in North Africa. The Japanese successfully bombed Darwin, Australia and, with overwhelming air, ground and naval power, were able to seize New Britain, New Ireland, the Admiralty Islands, the Gilberts and part of New Guinea. President Roosevelt knew that if the link with German forces was established, as it now appeared could happen, the Axis powers would be well on their way toward their ultimate goal of world domination.

President Roosevelt was desperate to take action, in order to give the American people hope in the war. He needed to strike back at the heart of Japan, and strike quickly, but the devastating attack on Pearl Harbor had effectively taken America out of the fight in the Pacific.

Roosevelt, and the Commanders of the Army, Navy and Air Corps, knew the only way to stop the Japanese expansion in the Pacific would be to bomb the Japanese mainland, which would cause them to withdraw some of their forces to defend their homeland. However, this meant that Admiral William "Bull" Halsey would have to sail his aircraft carriers within two hundred miles of Japan, for the Navy's carrier-based aircraft to reach their targets and safely return. The Japanese knew the limited range of America's naval aircraft, and had established a perimeter of naval forces along the coasts to stop the Americans from getting anywhere within striking distance of their country. The only American aircraft capable of long range bombing were the heavy bombers of the US Army Air Corps, but these aircraft were designed for land based operation and Japan now controlled all airfields within range of their country.

Whether by a stroke of luck or an act of Divine providence, a Navy officer happened upon an idea that eventually developed into a bold plan that would change the course of the war and military aviation. While checking on the status of the Navy's newest carrier, the *USS Hornet*, which was based at Norfolk, Virginia, Captain Francis Low noticed a carrier deck painted on the runway of the airfield, used by navy pilots to practice short distance takeoffs. While observing the air operations on the airfield, a flight of Army Air Corp twin engine bombers passed overhead on a practice bombing run. Watching the long range bombers fly over the simulated carrier deck gave Captain Low an idea, which he quickly reported to the Chief of Naval Operations, Admiral Ernest J. King. Could Army long range bombers be modified to take off on the limited runway of an aircraft carrier? If so, could the Navy get aircraft carriers in attack range of the Japanese mainland?

This idea put into motion one of the most secretive, daring and successful military aviation missions in American history.

However, such a mission would require a very special person to take command. There was only one aviator who would be daring enough to take on such a risky and dangerous mission, Lieutenant Colonel "Jimmy" Doolittle.

Doolittle was already a legend in Army aviation, being the holder of several aviation speed records. He was also the first aviator to fly coast to coast in less than twenty-four hours, and later broke his own record by accomplishing the same feat in less that twelve hours. He was a master mission planner who was not only fearless, but also incredibly brilliant. Without any hesitation, Doolittle was selected to mastermind this incredibly dangerous, but significantly important, mission.

For nearly two months, the Doolittle Raiders, as they would eventually be known, continuously trained for the mysterious mission. Then on March 23, Lt. Colonel Doolittle received a coded message from Washington that simply stated, "Tell Jimmy to get on his horse." This message, sent to both Navy and Army Air Corps personnel, was the secret code to immediately proceed with the mission. Upon receiving the message, Doolittle called together his volunteers and directed them to square away their belongings and take care of all personal business matters, as they would very soon be leaving Eglin Air Field.

The aircrews quickly took care of their personal matters, and said goodbye to family and friends, not knowing where they were going or how long they would be gone. Shortly thereafter, the crews flew their aircraft to McClellan Air Field in California, where they went through final tests and modifications. They were then flown to Alameda Field, where they were loaded onboard the *USS Hornet*.

On April 2, with sixteen B-25 Mitchell bombers and crews on board, the *Hornet* and its accompaniment of cruisers and destroyers, sailed under the Golden Gate Bridge, with only a few knowing that they were now bound for Japan. Not long after, the aircraft carrier *USS Enterprise*, with Admiral Halsey onboard, set sail from Pearl Harbor, with plans to rendezvous with the *Hornet* on April 12 at a predetermined point.

DESTINATION TOKYO

On April 17, the Mitchell B-25 bombers were ready; the crews had been advised of their mission only a few days earlier. Every one of the eighty airmen now knew their destination was the mainland of Japan; however, they also knew that to have enough fuel to complete the mission, they would have to launch within four hundred fifty miles of Japan.

Although the Mitchell Bombers had been modified to take off from the deck of the *Hornet*, they would not be able to land on the carrier. Their mission was to takeoff from the carrier once they were within range of the Japanese mainland, fly to their assigned targets in Japan, drop their lethal payloads on military and industrial targets, and continue on to China where they would land at friendly air fields. To avoid detection, in case the Japanese had radar, the aircrews would fly at extremely low altitudes, which would consume significantly more fuel. They were also advised that, after releasing their bombs over Japan, they would face a headwind all the way to China, which always blew west to east this time of year over the China Sea.

Everything had been calculated very carefully; the launching point, the headwind between Japan and China, even the weight and drag of the aircraft. If everything was to go as planned and the weather was good, the aircrews would have at least a favorable chance of completing the mission and making it far enough into China to avoid capture by the Japanese, who controlled much of the coastal areas. But there was no margin for error and everything would have to fall perfectly in place; otherwise, they would not have enough fuel to make it to safety.

Although still over two hundred miles from the planned launch point, Lt. Colonel Doolittle knew that they were now in the enemy's back yard, and the carrier task force was at great risk of being spotted by Japanese air patrols or fishing vessels. If detected before getting within four hundred fifty miles of Japan, they would either have to launch the aircraft early, or push the bombers into the sea to allow for the Navy fighters to be brought up from below to defend the task force. With the possibility that the mission could launch at any time, Doolittle decided to gather his aircrews to let them in on the final details of their historic mission.

After gathering the Raiders, their Commander once again gave them the opportunity to back out; but, none took the offer. Doolittle carefully explained that, if detected, they could have to launch earlier than planned. This idea concerned everyone, as the weather had taken a turn for the worse, and they were in the middle of what appeared to be a monsoon. Poor flying weather meant the possibility of strong headwinds, poor visibility and the burning of additional fuel, which was already a grave concern.

Before ending the meeting, Doolittle allowed the crews to ask questions. One of the pilots asked a question that was on the mind of every man in the meeting, "Colonel Doolittle, what should we do if we lose an engine or get hit by ack-ack fire and crash-land in Japan?"

Doolittle replied with a confidence and conviction that inspired each crewmember, "Each pilot is in command of his own plane when we leave the carrier. He is responsible for the decisions he makes for his own plane and his own crew. If you're separated, each of you will have to decide for yourself what you will do. Personally, I know exactly what I'm going to do."

Doolittle stopped speaking, leaving the room entirely silent, until another crewmember asked, "Sir, what will you do?"

"I don't intend to be taken prisoner," said Doolittle. "If my plane is crippled beyond any possibility of fighting or escaping, I'm going to bail my crew out and then drive it, full throttle into any target I can find where the crash will do the most damage. I'm forty-five years old and have lived a full life. Most of you are in your twenties and if I were you, I'm not sure I would make the same decision. In the final analysis, it's up to each pilot and, in turn each man to decide what he will do."

After the mission briefing dismissed, Sergeant Joe Manske returned to the flight deck to continue his task of checking out his aircraft. Joe, like many of the other mechanics, rarely left the aircraft since they had been moved into their final staging positions on the flight deck. He would often sleep on the deck near his aircraft, if the weather permitted.

On the evening of April 17, the weather turned from bad to worse; the task force was now facing excessive winds and rough seas. Thirty foot swells washed over the *Hornet's* deck, sending seawater rushing down the runway, threatening to wash anything not secured to the ship, into the ocean.

On the morning of April 19, Lt. Colonel Doolittle was on the bridge of the *Hornet* when one of the other ships signaled they had spotted a Japanese vessel about eleven miles out, and they believed the task force had been sighted by the enemy. The *USS Nashville* was ordered to sink the vessel, and the *USS Hornet* received the message: "Launch Planes. To Colonel Doolittle and Gallant Command. Good Luck and God Bless You"

Doolittle left the bridge and called to his men, "OK Fellas, this is it, Let's go!" At the same time, the ships klaxon sounded, followed by the announcement "Army personnel man your airplanes and take off immediately!"

Joe Manske hurried to the deck to begin the preparations for takeoff. His plane would be the fifth to depart, and he had to ensure both wing tanks and the special crawlway tank was filled with fuel. Manske had taken the crawlway tank out of the plane the day before to repair a leak, and refilled it with fuel. He filled the right wing tank while a sailor filled the left tank, but Manske did not double check the tank after the sailor finished. When the pilot, Captain Jones, ran through the startup procedure, he noticed the left tank was thirty gallons short, and ordered Mankse to top off the tank. A sailor passed him a fuel hose, but because the ship was at *battle stations*, all fuel pumps had been shut off.

By now the first plane, with Lt. Colonel Doolittle at the controls, was being readied for takeoff. As the lead plane in the line of sixteen B-25s, crammed closely together on the deck, Doolittle had the shortest amount of available runway, only about four hundred fifty feet. All eyes were on the lead plane, as Doolittle moved his throttles to full power and rolled toward the end of the carrier's deck. With a thirty knot headwind, Doolittle's plane lifted into the air with runway to spare.

The second and third planes also successfully departed, and now it was time for Captain Jones to start his engines. Several naval personnel on deck were yelling for Jones to get going, so he ordered Manske back into the plane and started the engines.

At the direction of one of the deckhands, Captain David Jones revved the engines and taxied his B-25 into position on a specially painted line that ran the length of the runway. With only six feet of clearance between the planes right wing and the ship's tower, Jones would have to keep his left wheel on the line to avoid hitting the tower and ripping off his right wing.

Jones and the other pilots had practiced numerous short field takeoffs during their special training for this mission. But this would be his first real carrier takeoff, and now he not only had to concentrate on keeping the plane from hitting anything on the deck, but his takeoff had to be timed so that he reached the end of the deck as the ship was on top of one of the huge waves; otherwise, he may get airborne only to fly into a rising wall of seawater.

As the *Hornet's* deck crew pulled the chocks from under the wheels of the bomber, Jones pressed heavily on the breaks. He then turned to a navy signalman, Lieutenant Edgar G. Osborne, and gave him a thumbs-up, indicating that all instruments were in the "green" and the aircraft and crew were ready for takeoff. Osborne began swinging a checkered flag in a large circle, a signal for Jones to advance the throttles forward. Jones, pressing firmly on the brakes, pushed both throttles to full power. As the brakes strained to hold back the powerful aircraft, Osborne began swinging the flag in faster and faster circles.

Co-pilot, Lieutenant Ross "Hoss" Wilder kept his eyes forward, looking down the short runway, as the carrier pitched downward and the spray from another wave came blowing over the bow. Water rushed down the deck toward the plane as deckhands held on to keep from being washed into the sea or a spinning propeller. Just as the ship began pitching upward, Osborne signaled to "go!" Jones released the brakes and the B-25 began slowly moving down the runway.

To Jones, it appeared as though the plane would fly right into the middle of one of the massive waves, but as they progressed down the flight deck, the bow began to rise. Osborne's signal to "go" was carefully timed so that when they reached the end of the runway, the ship's bow would be high upon a wave. At least that had worked for the first four aircraft that proceeded Captain Jones and his crew. However, Jones knew that there were too many factors in this operation that had to go just right and the takeoff would prove to be the easiest part of this mission. As the aircraft reached its minimum takeoff speed, Jones pulled slightly back on the yoke, and the B-25 lifted off the carrier's deck and into the air.

The navigator, Lieutenant Eugene McGurl, called out coordinates, and Captain Jones and Co-Pilot, Lieutenant Ross Wilder, set a course for the mainland of Japan. By nine twenty in the morning, the last of the sixteen planes had left the USS Hornet. Now Lt. Colonel Doolittle and his Raiders were all alone, in enemy territory.

Around twelve fifteen in the afternoon, the lead plane piloted by Lt. Colonel Doolittle had reached the Island of Japan and had the city of Tokyo in its sites. Doolittle climbed to an altitude of twelve hundred feet, lined up with a factory, and released his bombs. Within a short time, the other Raiders would follow, striking pre-selected targets across the Island of Japan. Amazingly, the Raiders met little resistance. While there was some anti-aircraft fire, it was much less than expected, and they were surprised at the lack of fighter aircraft, which had been expected in much greater numbers. After releasing their bombs, every pilot dove down to treetop level until they reached the ocean where they set a course directly towards China.

CHANGING WINDS

Once clear of the danger of anti-aircraft fire and out of the range of enemy fighter aircraft, the crews began calculating their remaining fuel. Doolittle's navigator, Lieutenant Henry A. Potter, advised that with the current headwind, they would run out of fuel one hundred thirty-five miles before reaching the Chinese coast. Navy meteorologists had warned the Raiders about the seasonal headwinds over the China Sea, and this was factored into the mission planning. However, due the premature launch of the mission adding nearly two hundred miles to their flight plans, and the unforeseen bad weather, they were quickly burning their remaining fuel.

Doolittle's co-pilot later recalled that, upon realizing their desperate situation, every crewmember aboard the plane began to pray. Doolittle ordered his crew to prepare the aircraft for crash landing in the water, and as he later remembered, "We began to make preparations for ditching. I saw sharks basking in the water below and didn't think ditching among them would be very appealing."

Every aircraft on this mission was in the same situation, low on fuel, deep in enemy territory, and facing a perilous headwind.

The ninth aircraft, piloted by Lieutenant "Doc" Watson, had developed a fuel leak in one of the special auxiliary tanks. Already lower on fuel than the other aircraft, Lieutenant Watson attempted to conserve fuel by throttling back the engines. At one point ,they were flying so slow with the nose pitched so high in the air, the crew was afraid the tail of the aircraft would drag the water. Lieutenant Watson continued this unusual flying until they came upon three Japanese Navy cruisers, which began firing on them. Only when the shells started hitting the water around them, did Lieutenant Watson throttle up and gain altitude. Lieutenant Watson, as every other pilot on this mission, had only one thing on his mind; fuel consumption.

On aircraft number five, Captain Jones and his entire crew were also gravely concerned about fuel. Sergeant Joe Manske, had not thought much about their fuel consumption earlier in the flight, nor had he seriously considered the thirty gallons of fuel they were short in the left wing tank. The excitement of getting airborne, navigating to the target, avoiding detection and delivering their payload kept his mind occupied. However, now that he and his fellow Raiders had time to think, they realized that without some type of miracle, they would not make it to China. It was then that Sergeant Manske, who had been raised in a good Christian home, knew he had only one hope. Manske decide it was time to turn their situation over to the only One who could help them now. Manske unbuckled his harness and, in the back of the Mitchell B-25 bomber, got down on his knees and prayed. Pilots, copilots, gunners, navigators and bombardiers in every plane were in the same predicament, and many of them were also seeking Divine intervention through prayer.

The Raiders were not the only ones praying for deliverance from their situation. Over five thousand miles away, in Madres, Oregon, Mrs. Hulda Andrus, the mother of Corporal Jacob DeShazar, the bombardier in aircraft number sixteen, was suddenly awakened with a burden to pray. Mrs. Andrus prayed until she felt the burden subside. She did not know about the raid, or that her son, at that very moment, was in an airplane on the other side of the world that was quickly running out of fuel. She just sensed something was wrong and she needed to pray.

While Sergeant Manske, other Raiders, and unknown numbers back home were praying, the crew aboard Doolittle's plane continued making preparations to ditch in the ocean. Then a miraculous event occurred. Lieutenant Colonel Doolittle later recalled the providential turn of events, "Fortunately, the Lord was with us. What had been a headwind slowly turned into a tailwind of about twenty-five miles per hour and eased our minds about ditching."

One by one, each plane began being pushed along by a tailwind that, according to Navy meteorologists, never occurred this time of year. Now every man had a renewed hope of at least making it to land. Indeed, just as Doolittle had stated, the Lord was with the Raiders.

In fact, the Lord had been with the Raiders from the very beginning of this mission. Unknown to anyone in the task force, on April 10 the Japanese had intercepted communications between the *Hornet* and the *Enterprise* and knew that Halsey's carriers were sailing toward Japan. The Japanese assumed that the Americans intended to attack Japan, and were attempting to sail within range of the mainland. Based on the location of the task force, the Japanese had correctly calculated that the task force would not be in position to launch an attack any earlier than April 18. This would not only give the Japanese time to prepare their defenses but, if they could locate Halsey's fleet, they could attack and sink the carriers, which would virtually eliminate American Naval power in the Pacific.

On April 16, the Japanese began launching long range aircraft to search and locate the American fleet. However, as it would later be revealed, the storms that began pounding the task force around that time had provided a protective cloud cover that hid them from Japanese search planes.

Another providential occurrence was the forceful winds, which were a welcome blessing to the pilots as they were taking off on the carrier's short runway; but these strong winds also separated the Raiders as they made their way to Japan, pushing several of the planes slightly off course. This caused the aircraft to arrive over their targets at different times, and from different directions. This would prove to be a perfect *unplanned* strategy, as it confused the anti-aircraft gunners, who could not predict from which direction the next attackers would come.

Further, the premature launch of the mission was also an act of God. Unknown to anyone in the task force, the Japanese had staged a planned air-raid drill on the morning of the attack. The drill had ended shortly before the first plane arrived over Tokyo, and everyone was just returning to their normal activities. Military personnel who had been at their anti-aircraft guns were making their way back to their barracks, and the Japanese fighter aircraft, now low on fuel, had just landed at their bases. When the air raid sirens sounded again, most assumed it was a part of the planned exercise and, only a very few immediately responded.

As a result of American ingenuity, the bravery of the Raiders, and a series of providential acts, the Raid on Japan was a success. Fifteen aircraft made it into China or crash landed along the Chinese coast. Seventy two Raiders were able to make it safely into the hands of allied nations, and return to duty. Three Raiders died as a result of bailing out of their planes, or drowning after crashing off the coast. Nine Raiders were turned over to the Japanese Army by unfriendly Chinese, and were taken prisoner. Three of these were executed as war criminals by the Japanese, and two died as a result of mistreatment while prisoners of war. Four of the captured Raiders survived the torture and mistreatment of the Japanese prisons, and were rescued by US commandoes near the end of the war.

Due to an engine in aircraft number eight burning excessive fuel, the pilot, Lieutenant Edward "Ski" York, determined they would never make it to China, so he diverted to Russia, where he successfully landed at a Russian airfield. He and his crew were involuntarily held by the Russians for over a year, until they were able to escape into Iran and eventually make it back to the United States.

The Raid on Tokyo had successfully forced the Japanese to pull back many of their forces, in order to defend their homeland from future air assault. The mission performed by Doolittle's Raiders stands as one of the most daring and successful operations in military aviation history. The bravery of the Raiders, their commitment to the mission, and their prayers, changed the course of World War II in the Pacific.

REFERENCES

Goldstein, Donald M. and Dixon, Carol Aido Deshazer, *Return of the Raider, A Doolittle Raider's story of War and Forgiveness*. Lake Mary, Florida; Creation House, 2010

Bradley, James, *Flyboys, A True Story of Courage*. New York, New York: Little Brown and Company, 2003

Glines, Carroll, V. *The Doolittle Raid, America's daring first strike against Japan*. Atglen, Pennsilvania: Shiffer Publishing Ltd.

Cohen, Stan. *East Wind Rain, A Pictorial History of the Pearl Harbor Attack*. Missoula, Montana: Pictorial Histories Publishing Company.

Glines, Carroll, V. *Four Came Home, The gripping story of the survivors of Jimmy Doolittles two lost crews*. Missoula, Montana: Pictorial Histories Publishing Company.

5

PLANNING, WORKING, AND PRAYER

General George Patton (1944)

"Give ear, O Lord, unto my prayer; And attend to the voice of my supplications. In the day of my trouble I will call upon thee: For thou wilt answer me."
Psalm 86:6-7

It was cold, bitterly cold; in fact it was downright freezing for the men of the United States Army's 106th Infantry Division. It was early morning on December 16, 1944 and the young soldiers were just beginning their sixth day on the front lines, in a remote and densely forested area of Belgium known as the Ardennes.

A sergeant, who had been standing watch throughout the night, tried to heat a cup of coffee by holding it over the burning cardboard cover of his "C" rations. He was anxiously awaiting dawn, but it was only five o'clock in the morning and the sun would not break over the horizon for at least another two hours. Daylight would not bring warmth, as the sun would once again be obscured by a solidly overcast sky that blocked its heat from reaching the freezing men. But dawn would bring light, which would allow him to see what the Germans were doing on the other side of the lines. Although the sergeant had been told the German Army did not have adequate ammunition, supplies, or troops along this area of the western front, he still felt better when he could see what was happening.

For several days the weather had been the same; cold, overcast, with an almost constant snowfall, but there were only nine more days until Christmas and they all knew that World War II in Europe was virtually over. A month earlier, rumors had circulated throughout the Army that, with the incredible speed in which the Allies were pushing through Europe, the war would soon be over and most American troops would be home by Christmas.

Since hitting the shores of Normandy on D-Day, the Allies had advanced so quickly, they outran their supply lines and had to rely on the Air Corps to resupply their troops on the front. With several days of completely overcast skies, dense fog, rain, and snow, all aircraft were grounded and, without airdrops of ammunition and supplies to the front lines, the advance had come to a dead halt.

Another obstacle slowing down the Allied advance was the German Army's position. During the advance, the German Army had been driven back to the old Siegfried Line where there were plenty of concrete bunkers and other defensive fortifications. Without Army Air Corp bombers to dislodge the Germans from their reinforced bunkers, General Dwight D. Eisenhower, the Supreme Allied Commander in Europe, established a "broad-front" strategy, placing American and British infantry units along the western front to keep the "krauts" at bay until the weather improved and the advance could resume.

The "broad-front" strategy established a defensive line which extended from the North Sea coast of the Netherlands, through Belgium, Luxembourg and France, ending at the northern border of Switzerland. This strategy required massive resources of supplies and soldiers to cover such a broad front line, and new infantry units, recently arrived from the United States, were brought forward to augment the more experienced combat units.

YOUNG AND INEXPERIENCED

The 106th Infantry Division was one of the units that was, literally, fresh out of training. Only two months earlier, they were still at Camp Miles Standish in Massachusetts, preparing to board the cruise ship *Queen Elizabeth* for their trip across the Atlantic. Arriving in England, they trained until they received orders to cross the English Channel and make their way to Belgium, where they were to relieve the embattled Second Infantry Division, one of the units being sent to the rear for some desperately needed rest and supplies.

Allied intelligence believed this portion of the Ardennes was the least likely place that any action would occur, so naturally this is where headquarters placed its least experienced units. This deployment would not only make the 106th Division the newest and least experienced unit on the western front, but they were also the youngest division in the entire Army, with the average age of the soldiers being only twenty-two years old.

With the Ardennes considered the "quiet front," the men of the 106th were spread extremely thin. Normally, a division would be expected to defend a line that extended about five miles, but the 106th was spread out along a section that extended over twenty-five miles. Even without combat experience, the men of the 106th knew how vulnerable they were; however, headquarters assured them there was no strategic advantage for the Germans to strike along this section of the front. The terrain was too rugged for a massive counter strike, and there were too few roads to gain a strategic advantage; nevertheless, knowing the German Army was only a few miles away had the men of the 106th, most of whom had never fired their rifles at anything other than training targets, a bit on edge.

The sergeant was extremely nervous about their current situation. Other than what amounted to a few short naps, he had not slept since they took their position six days earlier. But as headquarters had predicted, everything remained relatively quiet on both sides of the line; in fact, they rarely saw any unusual enemy activity or detected any appreciable troop movements or buildup of forces.

The only moment of excitement, thus far, had come a few days earlier when a gunner in the 422nd Regiment suddenly let loose with a barrage of .50 caliber machine gun fire, sending soldiers scrambling for cover. Within a few seconds the firing ceased and, to the relief of everyone, there was no return fire from the German side. A quick investigation revealed that the soldier was bored and decided to practice his marksmanship on a deer that had wandered into his line of fire.

SURPRISE ATTACK

As the thousands of men along the western front anxiously awaited sunrise, they were unaware that only a short distance away, concealed by the thick forest, over 250,000 German soldiers were quietly moving into position. They were also unaware that two thousand artillery cannons had been secretly moved into position and were, at that moment, aimed directly at the American positions along the Ardennes. Even in the stillness of the early morning, none of the American soldiers heard any of the fourteen hundred Panzer tanks hidden among the trees, as they fired up their engines. But before the day was over, the young and inexperienced men of the 106th Division would see and hear more combat action than most veteran Army units experienced throughout the war.

It began with a bright flash of light; then a shock wave hit the sergeant like an invisible fist, knocking the coffee cup out of the his hand. It was followed by a deafening roar and the dark morning sky lit up in bright yellow and red flashes, as more shock waves slapped at the soldiers. Stunned by surprise, as well the concussion of shells exploding all around, the sergeant lay motionless on the ground where he had fallen. Coming to his senses, he began shouting orders, but his men were already taking cover in their trenches and fox holes. Soldiers gripped their rifles, ready to take aim and fire, but there was nothing for them to shoot at, at least not yet.

The Germans were unleashing a tremendous artillery barrage on the American positions along a sixteen mile front extending north from where the 106th Division was entrenched. This same scenario was being experienced by the Fourteenth Cavalry Group and the Ninety-ninth Infantry Division, who held positions just north of the 106th. Back at Division headquarters, radios came alive with a constant chatter from the front. At five-fifty in the morning, the 443rd Anti-Tank Company reported they were "being shelled by Artillery since 0530 hours." The Ninety-ninth Infantry Division headquarters received similar reports from their front line elements, as they reported they were "taking heavy shelling all along the sector."

Artillery shells hit the ground exploding in rapid succession, sending fireballs of dirt, mud and rock flying in every direction. Occasionally, a shell would strike a vehicle, creating a tremendous explosion and throwing deadly shards of metal and glass into the air. But equally as treacherous were the shells that exploded in the treetops, hurling fragments of splintered wood into trenches and foxholes.

The bombardment continued for hours and then, just as abruptly as it had started, it suddenly ended. Cautiously, soldiers began to emerge from the safety of their trenches, and medics quickly responded to cries from the wounded. The battlefield returned to quiet, but the peace would only last for a moment, as the 106th and her sister units stood directly in the path of the largest German counter-attack of World War II. Before long, the spearhead of the German counter offensive would drive through the weakly defended American lines, decimating the 106th Infantry Division. Before the week was over, the 106th would see more than six hundred killed, nearly 1,250 injured, and over seven thousand missing or captured. In three days of brutal fighting, the 106th Infantry Division would virtually disappear; but not before her young, inexperienced soldiers would prove their mettle by slowing the Germans progress long enough for reinforcements to be moved forward into, what Winston Churchill named, *The Battle of the Bulge.*

BASTOGNE

By mid morning the first day of the battle, reports of enemy activity in the Ardennes sector began to filter into the Supreme Headquarters Allied Expeditionary Force (SHAEF) in Reims, France. General Eisenhower, who was celebrating his promotion to General of the Army, was informed of the action, and he immediately called his subordinate commanders together. By early afternoon, Eisenhower received notice that the Germans had completely broken through the line in the Ardennes, and were pushing through village by village. Except for a few units, who were heroically holding their positions, most American units were in a hasty retreat to the rear, in what the GIs called "the great bug-out." The 594th Engineering Battalion, Eisenhower was informed, had held out in the town of Malmady, to prepare bridges for demolition, set traps and establish road blocks, in an attempt to slow the Panzer tanks.

Some of Eisenhower's subordinate commanders dismissed the idea that this was an all out offensive move by the Germans, arguing that it was no more than isolated attacks on American positions. By late afternoon; however, a document taken from a German officer was delivered to the SHAEF headquarters. It was the "Order of the Day" issued by Field Marshall Gerd von Rundstedt, which confirmed that a major counteroffensive, to drive a wedge between the American and British Armies, was underway.

There were few roads in the Ardennes on which the German's tanks could travel, which made it easy to identify the two towns that were vital in stopping the German advance, Saint Vith and Bastogne. The German armored columns would have to pass through both towns to reach the bridgeheads over the Meuse River, and Eisenhower knew both had to be reinforced and held at all cost. With the weather prohibiting airlifting reinforcements from England, Eisenhower's only option was to redeploy his two Airborne Divisions, the 101st and 82nd. Both were in Reims being refitted after the fierce fighting they had encountered in Holland in September. Both Divisions were experienced combat units, but they were only lightly armed, and neither was adequately equipped for an extended ground combat operation; however, they were Eisenhower's only option, so he placed both divisions on alert, pending orders to move out quickly.

On December 17, the second day of the *Battle of the Bulge*, General Anthony McAuliffe, acting commander of the 101st Airborne Division, received orders from Eisenhower to "move your Division forward into Bastogne and hold the village at all costs." General McAuliffe loaded his division on trucks and raced towards Bastogne, arriving on December 18, just as the Germans began their siege.

Eisenhower knew that McAuliffe, who was now totally surrounded by German Panzer tanks, could not hold Bastogne for long. He called on General George Patton, whose Third Army was located about seventy five miles south of Bastogne along the Saar River, to mobilize three of his Divisions and relieve Bastogne. Patton, who was a lifelong scholar of warfare, had already devised plans to cut off the German advance, and immediately began mobilizing. But it would still take several days for Patton to reach the besieged town of Bastogne; and, unless the weather cleared, allowing the Air Corps to resupply, it was doubtful the 101st could hold out until Patton arrived.

Throughout the Ardennes, the Germans moved forward meeting little resistance, and thousands of American soldiers were being killed, wounded or captured. Remnants of units, who were cut off and surrounded by Germans, were held up in small towns, villages and farmhouses. Without reinforcements or supplies, the only thing the Americans could do was dig in, hold on and pray the weather would soon clear.

The weather was part of the German battle plan, and they were relying on the poor conditions to keep the American air forces grounded. It was the bad weather that allowed them to assemble their forces without detection, and to drive through the American lines like a hot knife through butter. As long as the weather remained unchanged, the Germans stood a good chance of reaching their objective, to occupy and hold bridges along the Muse River; and meteorologists on both sides did not foresee any change for several days.

PATTON'S PRAYER CARD

The weather had been a source of frustration for General George Patton for several weeks prior to the German invasion. Providentially, on the morning of December 8, several days before the Germans launched their surprise offensive, the Third Army Chaplain, Master Sergeant James H. O'Neill, unexpectedly received a call from the Third Army Commander. "This is General Patton," the voice on the other end of the line uttered, "Do you have a good prayer for weather? We must do something about those rains if we are to win the war." Chaplain

O'Neill assured the General that he would have a written prayer within the hour.

The Chaplain stood at his window and looked out at the steadily falling rain, which had hampered their operations for weeks. Since none of his prayer books included a prayer for weather, especially a prayer for good weather for battle, he sat down and wrote one himself.

Almighty and most merciful Father we humbly beseech Thee, of Thy great goodness, to restrain these immoderate rains with which we have had to contend. Grant us fair weather for Battle. Graciously hearken to us as soldiers who call upon Thee that, armed with Thy power, we may advance from victory to victory, and crush the oppression and wickedness of our enemies and establish Thy justice among men and nations.

Chaplain O'Neill typed the prayer on an index card and, on the reverse side, also wrote a Christmas message from the General.

Delivering the "prayer card," the Chaplain waited as General Patton read the prayer. Returning the card to the Chaplain, Patton ordered him to "have 250,000 copies printed and see to it that every man in the Third Army gets one." Just as O'Neill was preparing to leave, General Patton stopped him and said, "Chaplain, sit down for a moment; I want to talk to you about this business of prayer."

General Patton began to inquire of O'Neill as to whether or not the men of the Third Army had been praying. Somewhat surprised by this question, the Chaplain explained that when the soldiers are engaged in battle, everyone prays, but with the weather halting the advancement, the men mostly just sit around and wait. General Patton, who had been gazing out the window of his office, returned to his chair and sat down. With an air of sincerity and genuine concern for his men, he began to talk about the power of prayer.

"Chaplain, I am a strong believer in Prayer. There are three ways that men get what they want; by planning, by working, and by praying. Any great military operation takes careful planning, or thinking. Then you must have well-trained troops to carry it out: that's working. But between the plan and the operation there is always an unknown. That unknown spells defeat or victory, success or failure. It is the reaction of the actors to the ordeal when it actually comes. Some people call that getting the breaks; I call it God. God has His part, or margin in everything, that's where prayer comes in. Up to now, in the Third Army, God has been very good to us. We have never retreated; we have suffered no defeats, no famine, no epidemics. This is because a lot of people back home are praying for us… But we have to pray for ourselves, too… Great living is not all output of thought and work. A man has to have intake as well. I don't know what you call it, but I call it Religion, Prayer, or God."

Patton spoke of Gideon, and other Biblical characters, who prayed for God's intervention and witnessed miraculous answers to their prayers. Chaplain O'Neill responded in agreement, and informed the General that one of his objectives was to encourage prayer among the troops. General Patton then responded with an additional request,

"I wish you would put out a training letter on this subject of prayer to all the Chaplains; write about nothing else, just the importance of prayer... If we all pray... it will be like plugging in on a current whose source is in Heaven. I believe that prayer completes that circuit. It is power!"

The General ended the meeting, and Chaplain O'Neill returned to his office where he immediately began drafting the training letter that, accompanied by Patton's prayer card, would ultimately change the course of a battle that was yet to be fought.

The next day, Chaplain O'Neill called upon General Patton to approve the letter. General Patton took the letter and, after reading it thoroughly, ordered that it should be distributed to not only all four hundred eighty-six Chaplains, but to every organizational commander down to and including regimental commanders. Three thousand two hundred copies of "Training Letter Five" were distributed throughout the Third Army, encouraging prayer. This remarkable and providential letter read,

At this stage of the operations I would call upon the chaplains and the men of the Third United States Army to focus their attention on the importance of prayer.

Our glorious march from the Normandy Beach across France to where we stand, before and beyond the Siegfried Line, with the wreckage of the German Army behind us should convince the most skeptical soldier that God has ridden with our banner. Pestilence and famine have not touched us. We have continued in unity of purpose. We have had no quitters; and our leadership has been mas-

terful. The Third Army has no roster of Retreats. None of Defeats. We have no memory of a lost battle to hand on to our children from this great campaign.

But we are not stopping at the Siegfried Line. Tough days may be ahead of us before we eat our rations in the Chancellery of the Deutsches Reich.

As chaplains, it is our business to pray. We preach its importance. We urge its practice. But the time is now to intensify our faith in prayer, not alone with ourselves, but with every believing man, Protestant, Catholic, Jew, or Christian in the ranks of the Third United States Army.

Those who pray do more for the world than those who fight; and if the world goes from bad to worse, it is because there are more battles than prayers. 'Hands lifted up,' said Bossuet, 'smash more battalions than hands that strike.' Gideon of Bible fame was least in his father's house. He came from Israel's smallest tribe. But he was a mighty man of valor. His strength lay not in his military might, but in his recognition of God's proper claims upon his life. He reduced his Army from thirty-two thousand to three hundred men lest the people of Israel would think that their valor had saved them. We have no intention to reduce our vast striking force. But we must urge, instruct, and indoctrinate every fighting man to pray as well as fight. In Gideon's day, and in our own, spiritually alert minorities carry the burdens and bring the victories.

Urge all of your men to pray, not alone in church, but everywhere. Pray when driving. Pray when fighting. Pray alone. Pray with others. Pray by night and pray by day. Pray for the cessation of immoderate rains, for good weather for Battle. Pray for the defeat of our wicked enemy whose banner is injustice and whose good is oppression. Pray for victory. Pray for our Army, and Pray for Peace.

We must march together, all out for God. The soldier who 'cracks up' does not need sympathy or comfort as much as he needs strength. We are not trying to make the best of these days. It is our job to make the most of them. Now is not the time to follow God from 'afar off.' This Army needs the assurance and the faith that God is with us. With prayer, we cannot fail.

Be assured that this message on prayer has the approval, the encouragement, and the enthusiastic support of the Third United States Army Commander.

With every good wish to each of you for a very Happy Christmas, and my personal congratulations for your splendid and courageous work since landing on the beach.   *... signed The Third Army Commander*

Copies of "Training Letter Five" along with General Patton's prayer for good weather and the Christmas message, were distributed throughout the Third Army. Two days later, Patton received orders to relieve the beleaguered town of Bastogne.

OUR PRAYERS WORKED

With the distribution of Training Letter Five completed, and Patton's soldiers armed with a quarter of a million cards, with prayers for good weather, the Third Army began pushing full speed toward Bastogne.

On December 22, a German officer and two enlisted men approached the American lines holding a white flag of truce. They had a written message, addressed to the American military commander in Bastogne, from General von Lüttwitz. The message, which was immediately taken to General McAuliffe, informed him that Bastogne was completely surrounded by

German armored units and more reinforcements were on the way. To avoid "total annihilation" of the American troops and countless numbers of innocent civilians, the Germans would allow for the honorable surrender of the town and all the American forces in and around Bastogne. The letter, signed by Lüttwitz, gave McAuliffe two hours to consider the ultimatum, but McAuliffe did not need two hours to consider; he immediately responded by saying "Nuts," which was typed as the official response and returned to General Lüttwitz.

In response to the defiance of the American General, Lüttwitz ordered the Panzers to begin their assault immediately. Surrounded, under almost continual bombardment and critically low on ammunition, food, fuel and medical supplies, the situation looked incredibly grim for the 101st Airborne. With Patton still over a day away, it appeared that Bastogne would soon fall; but then, to the surprise of Allied meteorologists, and to the consternation of the German Army, the very next morning, the skies miraculously began to clear. The rain, fog, and snow dissipated and gave way to blue skies and, immediately, aircrews scrambled to their aircraft. While cargo planes dropped supplies and ammunition into Bastogne, Saint Vith, and the numerous places Americans were holding out, Allied fighters and bombers attacked German elements, destroying hundreds of Panzer tanks and halting the German advance.

For nearly a week Allied air forces enjoyed perfect flying weather and by the middle of January the invaders were driven back into Germany. The Battle of the Bulge was finally over and, although the last major German offensive of the war was very costly to the American forces, the Allied counter-offensive virtually destroyed the remaining elements of the German Army.

Master Sergeant O'Neill had not seen General Patton since he abruptly left to relieve Bastogne over a month and a half earlier. The two men finally met up again in late January, 1945 in the town of Luxembourg. Patton, upon seeing his Chaplain, hurried over, stood facing O'Neill, and with a big smile he said, "Well, Padre, our prayers worked. I knew they would." Patton then took his riding crop and cracked O'Neill on the side of his helmet. It was a friendly gesture, Patton's way of saying, "Well done."

REFERENCES

Cole, Hugh M. *The Ardennes: Battle of the Bulge.* Washington, D.C.: Center of Military History, U.S. Army, 1994. Print.

Cunningham, Paul E. *Freezing in Hell: World War II, Ardennes—Battle of the Bulge, December 16, 1944-January 25, 1945 : from the Foxhole Perspective of Soldiers in the 75th Infantry Division : over 200 First-hand Accounts by Men Who Were There.* [Salisbury, MD]: P.E. Cunningham, 1998. Print.

D'Este, Carlo. *Eisenhower: a Soldier's Life.* New York: Henry Holt &, 2002. Print.

D'Este, Carlo. *Patton: a Genius for War.* New York: HarperCollins, 1995. Print.

Lucas, James Sidney. *Command: a Historical Dictionary of Military Leaders.* New York: Military, 1988. Print.

O'Neill, James H. "*The Story Behind Patton's Prayer.*" Our Sunday Visitor, 15 Aug. 1971. Print.

O'Neill, James H. "*True Story of the Patton Prayer.*" Review of the News, 6 Oct 1971: pp. 29-40.

Patton, George Smith. *War as I Knew It.* Boston: Houghton Mifflin, 1975. Print.

Patton, George S., Jr. *War as I knew it: the battle memoirs of "Blood 'N Guts"* (Specially Illustrated Edition). New York, NY: Bantam Books, 1975. Print.

Sulzberger, C. L., David G. McCullough, and Ralph K. Andrist. *The American Heritage Picture History of World War II.* [New York]: American Heritage Pub., 1966. Print.

Whiting, Charles. *Patton.* New York: Ballantine, 1970. Print.

Whiting, Charles. *Siegfried: the Nazis' Last Stand.* New York: Stein and Day, 1982. Print.

6

THE SECOND GREATEST CHRISTMAS STORY

Crew of Apollo 8 (1968)

"In the beginning God created the heaven and the earth. And the earth was without form, and void; and darkness was upon the face of the deep. And the Spirit of God moved upon the face of the waters."

Genesis 1:1-2

The Mission Control Center at the Johnson Space Center near Houston, Texas was quiet. It was Christmas Eve, and even with the mass of activity in the Control Room and the adjacent observation area filled with guests, the area was almost totally quiet with nervous anticipation. The silence was occasionally interrupted by the voice of Capsule Communications Operator (CAPCOM) Gerry Carr, as he attempted to contact the crew of Apollo Eight, "Apollo 8, this is Houston, over." But as with previous attempts, his calls were only answered with the hiss of radio static. A few moments later, Carr once again leaned over to the microphone at his console and called, "Apollo 8, this is Houston, over." Again, there was no reply from the spacecraft that had carried the first humans out of Earth's orbit.

It had been almost thirty minutes since the Apollo 8 crew had slipped behind the Moon which, as expected, had cut off all communications between the crew and Earth. At three o'clock in the morning, Central Standard Time, December 24, 1968, Mission Control had transmitted to Apollo 8 that they were "Go" for Lunar Orbit Insertion (LOI), a maneuver that would put the spaceship in orbit around the Moon. LOI required the Apollo crew to fire their main engine to slow down the spacecraft enough so that it would be captured by the Moon's gravitational field.

During their three day trip between the Earth and the Moon, known as the Trans Lunar Coast (TLC), the Apollo 8 crew had turned the spacecraft around so it was flying backwards at nearly 25,000 miles per hour. The thrust of the main engine pushing in the opposite direction is how they would slow down, but the timing of the engine "burn" was carefully calculated, and had to be precise. Too long a burn would slow them too much and the spacecraft, with the three American astronauts on board, could crash into the surface of the Moon. Too short a burn could result in a slingshot effect, hurtling the spacecraft into the infinity of space. With only enough life support for a six day mission, the astronauts would die a slow and agonizing death from asphyxiation.

The only contingency the astronauts had, should anything go wrong, was to abort firing the engine, which would sling them around the Moon and put them on a return course back to Earth. But for the men onboard the spacecraft, this would be a last resort. Their mission was to make ten orbits around the Moon before returning to Earth, and they were determined to carry out their mission.

For the three days astronauts Frank Borman, Commander; William "Bill" Anders, Lunar Module Pilot; and Jim Lovell, Command Module Pilot, had been in space, they were in constant voice and data contact with Mission Control. Since lift off from Cape Canaveral in Florida, there had been several engine burns; one to get them into Earth's orbit, another to leave Earth's orbit and put them on a course to the Moon, and several minor burns to adjust their course headings. During each of these critical moments, the Apollo 8 spacecraft continually sent telemetry information back to Houston. Systems and navigational information transmitted back to Mission Control allowed the center's engineers and scientists to assist the crew in critical calculations and navigation. However, this LOI had to be conducted on the back side of the Moon, which meant there would be no communications, no help with calculation, no assistance from Mission Control. For the first time on their historic flight, the Apollo 8 astronauts were entirely on their own, alone in the vacuum of space a quarter of a million miles from Earth.

Back at Houston, everyone was anxious for some response from either the crew or the spacecraft's data feed. Two clocks in the Control Center were counting down the time since Loss of Signal (LOS). The first clock counted the time that it would take Apollo 8 to regain signal if they had aborted the LOI and were on their way back to Earth. The second clock counted down to the time they would regain signal if they had properly slowed down the spacecraft and were on the proper Lunar orbit.

As the first clock counted down to zero, controllers checked their computer screens to see if they were able to reacquire a data connection, but everything remained silent. Again Gerry Carr attempted to make radio contact "Apollo 8, this is Houston, over." The silence following his call, and the blank computer screens, meant that Apollo 8 had slowed down and at least attempted to enter Lunar orbit.

Outside the confines of the Johnson Space Center and all across the country, millions of American's, on this Christmas Eve, were consumed with last minute shopping, preparing Christmas meals or making travel plans. But at Mission Control, their thoughts were focused on the three men behind the Moon. Were their calculations correct? Were the Apollo 8 astronauts now orbiting sixty miles above the Moon's surface? Did the engine properly ignite? These and countless other questions were running through the minds of everyone in the Control room.

"Apollo 8, this is Houston, over," Carr continued, his calls now sounding more like prayers. The second countdown clock was nearing zero, and Carr began making his calls in fifteen second intervals.

"Apollo 8, this is Houston, over." Silence.

"Apollo 8, this is Houston, over." Still no reply.

Then suddenly, within one second of the reacquisition clock reaching zero, a controller announced, "Flight, we've had telemetry acquisition." A brief and reserved cheer broke out in the room, as everyone realized that the Apollo 8 spacecraft had regained data communications. A few seconds later, the voice of Frank Borman, Apollo 8 Mission Commander, broke the silence, "Go ahead, Houston. This is Apollo 8. Burn complete…"

"Apollo 8, this is Houston. Roger. Good to hear your voice," Carr responded, as the Control room and the observation area broke out in massive cheers and celebration. In a few short hours, Americans would awaken to the historic news that the first humans had traveled beyond the gravitational field of our own planet and were circling the Moon.

With the country involved in an unpopular war in Vietnam, violent war protests erupting at many college campuses across the nation, and the looming threat of nuclear war with the Soviet Union, Americans desperately needed a reason to be proud. Not since Christopher Columbus discovered the New World, had humans accomplished such a feat of discovery, and this time it was Americans exploring new worlds beyond the heavens.

For the first time, the United States leaped ahead of the Soviet Union in the space race, and the country was certainly poised and ready to celebrate. However, on board Apollo 8 it was all business. Their mission was only halfway completed, and there was still a lot of work to do before they could return to their home planet.

The success of the Apollo 8 mission was nothing short of a miracle. Only four months earlier, George Low, the Apollo program manager, accelerated the flight schedule, deciding that the original plans for Apollo 8 to test the CSM (Command and Service Modules) and Lunar Landing Module (LLM) in low Earth orbit would be scratched. Due to recent advancements in the Soviet Union's space program and the threat of budget cuts by Congress, NASA needed to get to the Moon faster than originally planned, so the Apollo 8 mission was changed. The crew of Apollo 8 would be the first humans to leave Earth's orbit, travel to and orbit the Moon.

When George Low proposed this change, it seemed impossible, especially since the proposed launch window was within four short months and the construction of the CSM had not been completed. The accelerated launch schedule would leave little time for testing the new Apollo *Saturn V* spacecraft, or to retrain the crew for a new mission. But American ingenuity, and the can-do, will-do attitude of those in the space program, kicked into gear and a launch date was set for December 21, 1968.

To meet the new launch schedule, numerous technical and logistical issues had to be overcome in a very short amount of time. Training schedules were readjusted for both astronauts and Mission Control personnel. The task of calculating the exact trajectories for entering and leaving Earth's orbit, intersecting the Moon as it orbits around the Earth, and getting the astronauts back home, was very complex. The team of mathematicians and physicists calculating the flight plans were given priority access to NASA's huge computer systems, which caused the rescheduling and postponing of other space flight operations. The simulators used for training the crews were reprogrammed for the new mission. Getting the crew of Apollo 8 to the Moon became the top priority, so everything in NASA was quickly reorganized to meet the new and aggressive launch schedule.

Preparing the crew for their historic flight fell on the shoulders of the Apollo 8 Commander, Frank Borman, who faced a myriad of technical and training difficulties. But it was another issue which seemed the toughest for him to resolve. An issue not even being considered by most at NASA, especially the hundreds of scientists and engineers working on the technical aspects of the mission; but it was significant to Borman.

With Apollo 8 scheduled to be in orbit around the Moon on Christmas Eve, the entire world would be watching and listening to their Christmas Eve broadcast, live from space. Borman's struggle was with what to say on such an important and historic occasion. What words would be appropriate for a worldwide audience, on the eve of a holiday celebrated by many of the world's cultures? The words he chose, right or wrong, inspiring or disappointing, would be recorded in the annals of history.

For weeks, Borman struggled over this issue. He consulted with NASA's Public Affairs office, hoping that they would have some official pre-written statement. However, their response was that it would be inappropriate for NASA, or its Public Affairs office, to put words in the mouths of the astronauts. This was clearly something that Borman had to figure out on his own.

As the launch date drew nearer, Frank Borman consulted the other members of the crew. They tossed around ideas ranging from making some statement about world peace, to rewriting the poem "T'was the Night Before Christmas," but none of these seemed to portray the significance of the occasion. Fellow crewman, Bill Anders suggested reading the Christmas story from the gospel of Luke, but after a lengthy discussion, they decided against that as well. Commander Borman reached out to his wife, his pastor and other friends, but none of their suggestions seemed totally appropriate.

As Borman continued to ponder the issue, the scientists, engineers and physicists continued preparing for the launch. NASA
had given little thought to the Christmas Day broadcast until a
press conference, just weeks before the launch, brought the significance of what the crew would say to light. During the press
conference, a reporter asked the astronauts if they would make a
"Christmas-type gesture from space." Borman, who rarely
lacked words, struggled with a response, and finally admitted
that they had not determined what they would say. Now many
at NASA, including the Public Affairs office, were suddenly anxious about the Christmas broadcast and what the astronauts
would say. The Public Affairs office realized that the Christmas
message, which would be the crew's second broadcast from the
Moon, would be the most listened to program in history. But
NASA's stance remained consistent, the astronauts would have
to determine what to say, and that responsibility rested squarely
on the shoulders of the mission's Commander.

As Apollo 8 continued its orbits around the Moon, Borman,
Anders and Lovell were busy analyzing the landscape of the
Lunar surface. One of their primary missions was to identify
possible landing locations for the forthcoming Lunar landing of
Apollo 11. They also made preparations for their first television
broadcast, which would begin on their second orbit, as soon as
they emerged from the back side of the Moon.

It was now five forty-five in the morning, as the Flight
Director, Milton Windler, gave the go-ahead for their second
orbit. CAPCOM radioed the crew, "Apollo 8, this is Houston.
All systems are Go. You're still Go for Rev two. Over." "Thank
You," replied Borman, as the crew began preparing the sixteen

millimeter television camera for the first television broadcast from the Moon.

As the spacecraft emerged from their second trip around, the camera was already rolling, and images of the stark grey Lunar landscape appeared on television sets around the world. Bill Anders began narrating the broadcast, describing the images they were viewing as he moved the camera between the two windows. Jim Lovell assisted Anders, identifying specific landmarks using a map of the Lunar surface. For eleven minutes, the world saw for the first time ever, a close up view of the surface of the Moon, televised by three incredibly brave American astronauts. This would be the last the world would hear from the Apollo 8 crew until their much awaited, and highly publicized, Christmas broadcast on their ninth orbit around the Moon later that evening.

As the Apollo 8 crew emerged from the backside of the Moon on their third orbit, astronaut Mike Collins was now seated at the CAPCOM console. It was around ten o'clock in the morning when Frank Borman called Houston with an unusual request.

"Mike, this is Frank again," Borman said; this time his voice had a more personal tone.

"Apollo 8, this is Houston…" Mike Collins replied.

"Is Rod Rose around?" asked Borman.

"Rod Rose is sitting up in the viewing room; he can hear what you say," replied Collins.

"I wonder if he is ready for experiment P1?" asked Borman.

Rod Rose gave a thumbs-up sign to Collins from behind the glass panel wall. Collins promptly radioed the response to

Borman. Then to the surprise of everyone, except Rod Rose, Borman began,

"This is to Rod Rose and the people at St. Christopher's, actually to people everywhere."

Then Borman began to pray:

Give us, O God, the vision which can see thy love in the world, in spite of human failure. Give us the faith to trust thy goodness in spite of our ignorance and weakness. Give us the knowledge that we may continue to pray with understanding hearts, and show us what each one of us can do to set forth the coming of the day of universal peace. Amen.

"Amen," echoed Collins.

Rod Rose was an engineer at NASA, and a member of the same church as Frank Borman. Before the Apollo 8 mission was rescheduled, Borman had committed to read scripture and pray at their church's Christmas Eve service. Being one who strongly believed in keeping his promises, Borman intended to follow through, so he arranged for Rose to record the prayer he would pray from space, and take the recording to the church to be played that evening.

"I was supposed to lay-read tonight, but I couldn't quite make it." Borman added.

"Roger. I think they will understand," replied Collins.

It was now late evening on Christmas Eve at the Mission Control Center in Houston. Apollo 8 was again on the back side of the Moon beginning their ninth orbit. The Mission Control Center was packed. This time Julian Scheer, NASA's Assistant Administrator for Public Affairs, was in the room, as well as several other VIPs and NASA officials. They came partly to witness the Trans Earth Injection (TEI), a critical maneuver conducted on the tenth orbit, which would accelerate them out of the Lunar orbit and send them back to Earth, but more importantly, they were there to witness what Commander Borman would say to the entire world this Christmas Eve. NASA officials had concluded that this would be the most watched television broadcast in the history of the world.

As the Apollo 8 spacecraft emerged from the "backside," televisions around the world came alive with images of the Earth as seen from 250,000 miles away. Frank Borman began the broadcast, "This is Apollo 8, coming to you live from the Moon." The Mission Control staff continued with their various tasks, paying little attention to the broadcast the rest of the world was intently watching. It was not that they were disinterested in the images of the Earth as the astronauts were seeing it. In fact, most in Mission Control had dedicated the past several years of their lives planning for this moment. Their hearts were definitely with the men circling the Moon, but their minds were focused on the critical task of getting the crew around the Moon one more time, and then safely back home to their families. Systems were being checked and cross-checked, trajectories were being verified, and weather in the Pacific Ocean was now a concern, and had to be closely monitored.

Onboard Apollo 8, Bill Anders moved the camera to the window facing the Moon, as Borman continued, "We showed you first a view of Earth as we've been watching it for the past sixteen hours. Now we're switching so that we can show you the Moon that we've been flying over at sixty miles altitude for the last sixteen hours. Bill Anders, Jim Lovell, and myself have spent the day before Christmas up here doing experiments, taking pictures, and firing our spacecraft engines to maneuver around."

Borman continued, explaining his thoughts and feelings about what they were experiencing. He then asked Jim Lovell to express his thoughts, and Lovell, in a deeply emotional tone, began his commentary.

"Well, Frank, my thoughts were very similar. The vast loneliness up here at the Moon is awe-inspiring, and it makes you realize what you have back there on Earth. The Earth from here is a grand oasis in the big vastness of space..."

Jim Lovell's comments were spoken with such emotion, it felt as if he were truly homesick for his home planet. Frank Borman now turned to Bill Anders and asked, "Bill, what do you think?"

The Mission Control Center was still buzzing with activity. Controllers moved about, paying little attention to the television monitors displaying incredible images of the grey and barren Lunar landscape. Anders continued, "I think the thing that impressed me the most was the Lunar sunrises and sunsets. These in particular bring out the stark nature of the terrain."

For several moments, the three astronauts continued their commentary on what they were seeing, feeling and experiencing, as the first humans to visit the Moon. They described the Moon's landscape in fascinating detail.

Then, Bill Anders paused as he reached for their flight plan and opened it to a special insert Borman had placed inside before liftoff. "We are now approaching Lunar sunset and for all the people back on Earth, the crew of Apollo 8 has a message that we would like to send to you."

Bill Anders again paused, and the activity in Mission Control suddenly ceased. This was the moment; this is what would be written in the history books of the world; this is what the entire planet would hear from the brave American explorers of the heavens. Once again, as when they had passed behind the Moon for the first time several hours earlier, Mission Control was totally quiet. All heads were turned upwards towards the video monitors, intently listening for the astronaut's next words. Some walked over and stood in front of a small television set, while others sat still at their consoles. Everyone's attention was focused on the three men circling the Moon, anxious to witness this historic statement.

Other than a couple of trusted individuals who would be working Mission Control that evening, no one at NASA knew what Commander Frank Borman planned to say. Those to whom Borman had confided were only told because he wanted them to know there would be a long pause at the conclusion of their remarks, and he wanted to maintain complete radio silence until they finally signed off.

Bill Anders began reading from the special page that had been tucked inside their flight plan. His voice was very soft and reverent. "In the beginning, God created the heavens and earth. And the earth was without form, and void; and darkness was upon the face of the deep."

As Anders passed the flight plan to Jim Lovell, those at Mission Control were struck with a sense of awe. No one spoke a word; they just watched and listened as Lovell continued, "And God said, 'Let there be a firmament in the midst of the waters, and let it divide the waters from the waters.' And God made the firmament and divided the waters which were under the firmament from the waters which were above the firmament. And it was so. And God called the firmament Heaven. And the evening and the morning were the second day."

Gene Kranz sat at one of the consoles in Mission Control. Gene would soon be recognized as a national hero as the Flight Director of the ill fated Apollo 13 mission. Kranz's famous words, "failure is not an option," would inspire thousands both inside and outside of America's space program. But at this moment Kranz sat at his console, mesmerized, with his full attention on the words emanating from another world 250,000 miles away.

Aboard the Apollo 8 spacecraft the flight plan was handed to Frank Borman, who continued the verses from the book of Genesis, "And God said, 'Let the waters under the heaven be gathered together unto one place, and let the dry land appear.' And it was so." Borman briefly paused and then reverently continued, "And God called the dry land Earth; and the gathering together of the waters called he Seas; and God saw that it was good."

Finishing with Genesis 1, verse 10, Commander Borman once again paused, this time longer than before. The Flight Director and CAPCOM sat quietly; no one moved or uttered a sound. And then, in a sincere and solemn tone, he concluded the television broadcast, heard by millions of people around the world, saying,

"And from the crew of Apollo 8. We close with good night; good luck, a Merry Christmas, and God bless all of you - all of you on the good Earth." With those words, Bill Anders turned off the television camera onboard Apollo 8 and millions of television sets across the Earth turned to static.

In Mission Control, everyone remained quiet as the voices of the astronauts faded, replaced by the slight hiss of radio static. Gene Kranz, with tears on his cheeks, said he felt as if the presence of 'Creation and the Creator' was in Mission Control with them.

On December 27, 1968, little more than two days following their historic broadcast, Frank Borman, Bill Anders and Jim Lovell climbed out of their capsule, now afloat in the Pacific Ocean, and America celebrated. Prior to the flight of Apollo 8, only God and the angels had seen the Earth and the heavens from the vantage point of these three men.

Frank Borman's message had touched millions, and though he had tried to invent some historic statement that would be fitting to the moment, and bring a sense of hope and peace to a troubled world; the more he tried, the more inadequate his own words had seemed. The words he chose on this historic moment were not written by the astronauts or the government, but they were written thousands of years earlier. They were not the words of man, but words inspired by the Creator; the One who created the vastness of space and the new worlds they were exploring.

Across the nations, people were inspired by this broadcast, but not everyone was pleased. Madelyn Murray O'Hair, who had successfully won a Supreme Court case resulting in removal of prayer from public schools, immediately complained to NASA about the reading of the Bible by the astronauts. She sent NASA a petition with over 28,000 signatures, demanding that in future space flights, astronauts be prohibited from making religious statements from space. But NASA's position was that the United States was a free society, and unlike the Soviet Union, which carefully scripted everything their cosmonauts transmitted from space, Americans had a right to free speech, and NASA would not dictate what the astronauts would say.

O'Hair filed suit against NASA to try to force censorship on future space flights, but over 2,500,000 Americans responded by sending NASA cards and letters supporting the Apollo 8 astronauts remarks, and their rights of free speech and religious expression. In the end, a federal judge dismissed the case, citing that even though astronauts were representatives of the United States, they were still afforded the same rights as all Americans.

Due to the commitment of Americans to the space program, and the courage of the Apollo 8 crew, the world had observed one of the greatest accomplishments of mankind, and witnessed an historic heartfelt message from the heavens which, as Gene Kranz would later state, "…was the second greatest Christmas Story ever told."

REFERENCES

Kranz, Gene. *Failure is Not an Option, Mission Control from Mercury to Apollo 13 and Beyond.* New York, New York; Simon and Schuster, 2000

Lee, Wayne. *To Rise from Earth, An Easy to Understand Guide to Spaceflight.* New York, New York; Checkmark Books, 2000

Murray, William J. *Let Us Pray, A Plea for Prayer in Our Schools.* New York, New York; William Morrow and Company, 1995

Zimmerman, Robert. *Genesis, The Story of Apollo 8,* New York, New York: Dell Publishing, 1999

Other References

Manned Spacecraft Center. *Apollo 8, Technical Air-To-Ground Voice Transcription.* Houston, Texas, 1968

7

STANDING FIRM

Private Desmond Doss (1945)

"Therefore, My beloved brethren, be steadfast, immovable, always abounding in the work of the Lord, knowing that your labor is not in vain in the Lord."
I Corinthians 15:58 (NKJV)

When the United States Army's 307th Infantry Regiment, part of the Seventy-Seventh Infantry Division, landed on Okinawa in April 1945, they were greeted by a most harrowing sight. Bodies of slain soldiers from the Ninety-Sixth Infantry Division, whom they had been sent to relieve, were being unloaded from trucks and stacked alongside the narrow roadway that led inland. As the men of the 307th struggled to haul their supplies and equipment through the sand and deep mud, another convoy of trucks bearing their gruesome payloads arrived. Some of the newly arriving soldiers stood in shock as

they observed teams of men grabbing the mangled and disfig-
ured bodies and heaving them into stacks.

The Ninety-Sixth Infantry Division had been part of the initial invasion of Okinawa which had landed nearly four weeks
earlier. Operation Iceberg, the codename for the Okinawa campaign, comprised the largest invasion force in history, a multi-
service force even larger than the one that stormed the beaches
of Normandy on D-Day almost a year earlier. Okinawa was the
next step towards an invasion of the Japanese mainland, and the
United States was throwing everything it had at the occupants
of this small narrow island. But the Japanese had no intention of
giving up their last bastion of security, and they were prepared
to vigorously defend the island. The Japanese were highly concealed and heavily armed. This, combined with their aggressive
and often suicidal tactics, had resulted in massive casualties for
the American forces.

The Japanese Army did not recognize nor honor any rules of
war; their only law of engagement was the total annihilation of
the enemy by whatever means necessary. There were numerous
accounts, during the battles of Guam and Leyte, of Japanese
snipers specifically targeting Army medics and Navy corpsmen.
They were also known to have gone onto the battlefields at
night to torture wounded soldiers. On one occasion, a group of
three Japanese soldiers bearing a white flag approached an
American position. The Americans, honoring the white flag of
truce, emerged from their protective cover to meet the
approaching soldiers. Once the Americans soldiers were out in
the open, the Japanese dropped their flag and hurled grenades
into their ranks, killing them all. From then on, American sol-

diers shot any Japanese approaching their position, white flag or not.

As part of the initial invasion force, the Ninety-Sixth Infantry Division had met little resistance when they first landed on Okinawa's northwestern shore. They easily took and held the beachhead and moved further inland with only minimal casualties, but that changed when they reached a four hundred foot high ridge called the *Madera Escarpment*. At the escarpment is where they met the full fury of the Japanese, and experienced just how well concealed and heavily armed the island's defenders really were. The hundreds of bodies, now stacked up on the beach, were the result of seven days of fierce fighting at the escarpment.

The Seventy-Seventh Infantry Division had been held in reserve aboard troop ships anchored off the coast of Okinawa during the initial invasion. Now sent to relieve their sister Division, the Seventy-Seventh were going to be active participants in this bloody battle. To the soldiers of the newly arriving Seventy-Seventh, who had already experienced combat with the Japanese on Guam and Leyte, the scene of hundreds of mangled bodies stacked like cordwood served as a warning for what awaited them further inland. For the newer replacements, who had recently arrived from the states, it was their first look at the true horrors of the war in the Pacific.

HACKSAW RIDGE

The Ninety-Sixth Infantry Division had suffered tremendous losses fighting at the Madera Escarpment, and the remnant was pinned down by the Japanese. On April 28 the Seventy-Seventh Infantry Division received orders to move inland and relieve what remained of the decimated Ninety-Sixth. Upon arriving at the escarpment, the Seventy-Seventh provided cover for the Ninety-Sixth, allowing them to safely withdraw. Once the Ninety-Sixth had pulled back, the Seventy-Seventh began making preparations to attack the Japanese positions located on the opposite slope of the escarpment. According to their maps, the official name of the obstacle before them was the Madera Escarpment, but to soldiers who had fought for days trying to dislodge the Japanese from its top, it was now called *Hacksaw Ridge.*

Hacksaw Ridge was a four hundred foot tall horseshoe shaped ridge that led to a flat plateau with a gradual reverse slope. The first three hundred fifty feet of the ridge was a steep and rocky incline. Climbing this portion of the cliff was rather difficult, but the soldiers were able to scale it without the use of ropes or ladders; however, the last forty to fifty feet, the ridge was a nearly vertical rock wall.

The Japanese, as the as the Americans experienced, had a definite advantage at Hacksaw Ridge. Having occupied the island for decades, they had carefully planned and constructed an impressive array of defensive fortifications. Through a network of heavily fortified and well supplied tunnels, the Japanese were able to wait out the artillery barrages and air raids that preceded the American infantry attacks. Once the American infantry began their assaults, the Japanese would emerge from their underground fortresses, attack their invaders and retreat back into their underground lair. Able to move around undetected, they would emerge at another location and attack again.

Each time the Americans launched an attack at Hacksaw Ridge, the Japanese would put up only minor resistance, allowing the Americans to ascend to the top of the ridge in large concentrations. Once the Americans were on top, the Japanese would emerge from their tunnels and unleash a barrage of mortar, machine gun and rifle fire, inflicting much injury and driving the Americans back down the ridge. Nine times in seven days, the Americans had taken Hacksaw Ridge; and nine times they had been driven back down.

The stalemate at the ridge was impeding the advancement of the American offensive, and the entire battle on the southern end of Okinawa became focused on this rocky cliff. The Japanese stronghold on the backside of the ridge had to be broken, thus the Seventy-Seventh Infantry Division was given orders to take control of Hacksaw Ridge.

The Commander of the 307th Infantry Regiment, Colonel Hamilton, sent short and simple orders to his unit commanders, "take and hold the ridge." Companies A and B of the 307th were selected to spearhead the attack. Surveying the ridge, Captain Vernon, the Commander of Company B, knew his men needed a better way to climb the fifty foot wall than the makeshift ladders that had previously been used. He sent a request to headquarters for cargo nets to be brought in from one of the troop carriers. His idea was to hang the nets from the top of the escarpment, which would allow the soldiers to climb the last fifty feet in mass. Captain Vernon surmised that, just as the nets were used to allow large numbers of soldiers to climb down from ships into landing craft, they could also be used to get soldiers to the top of the ridge.

When the nets arrived, Captain Vernon asked for volunteers to climb to the top and secure the nets. It was an extremely dangerous mission, as the top of the ridge contained several Japanese machine gun nests well within range, and snipers were always present. Three volunteers from Company B stepped forward. Among them was the company's medic, Private First Class Desmond T. Doss, who had seen plenty of action in both Leyte and Guam, and he fully understood the danger that awaited them at the top of the ridge. Desmond's volunteering was not a surprise to anyone, as he had proven his uncommon bravery during previous battles, and throughout his service, the men of the Seventy-Seventh had come to know that Private Doss was driven by a different set of principles than most.

Desmond Doss was a devout Christian who had joined the Army in early 1942 out of a pure desire to serve his country. Prior to his enlistment, Desmond had secured a good job at the Newport News Naval shipyards in Virginia. He was a hard worker and well liked by his superiors and peers. As Desmond was on his way to work on the morning of December 7, 1941, he heard news of the attack at Pearl Harbor broadcast over his car radio. Following the United State's Declaration of War, Desmond was notified that he had been selected for the draft, and would soon have to report for military service.

Desmond immediately notified his supervisor, so the company could begin looking for someone to fill his position. The supervisor advised Desmond that his job was in direct support of the war effort, and this qualified him for a deferment. "You know you are working in an essential industry," he told Desmond, "we could try to get you on the deferred list. With so many of our workers going into the Army, we are already short-handed..." However, to the supervisor's surprise, Desmond declined the offer. His supervisor tried to appeal to Desmond's strong sense of patriotism, explaining that, by taking a deferment, he would still be serving his country, helping the war effort here at home. Desmond replied, "My health is good; and I don't believe I am any better than the other fellows who are going in." Thanking the supervisor for the offer, Desmond respectfully declined, and when the assigned date arrived, Desmond reported to the draft board and was shipped off to Camp Lee, Virginia for his induction into the U. S. Army.

Shortly after arriving at Camp Lee, Desmond faced the first of many challenges he would encounter throughout his service. The bus of new recruits arrived at Camp Lee late on a Friday afternoon, too late to begin the induction process. Since they were not officially in the Army until the induction process was complete, they were given one last evening of liberty. While many of the recruits headed out to hit local restaurants, bars and theaters, Desmond found a local church and attended their Friday evening service.

The next morning Desmond arose early because he intended on attending services at one of the local Adventist churches. As a member of the Seventh-day Adventist Church, Desmond strictly observed Saturday as the Sabbath, God's commanded day of rest. However, as soon as he and the other recruits finished their breakfast, a sergeant burst into the room and announced there would be an inspection later in the day. "That means you are going to get these barracks clean," he bellowed. As he continued belching out orders, Desmond approached the sergeant. "Sergeant, sir," Desmond said getting his attention, "I am a Seventh-day Adventist, and today is my Sabbath. I can't do that kind of work on Sabbath."

The sergeant turned to Desmond and hollered, "You're what? What on earth is a Seventh-day Adventist and why can't you help with the cleaning, mama's boy?" The other recruits chuckled as the sergeant chastised Desmond for what they thought was a ridiculous request. "I am not afraid to clean," said Desmond, "but I can't do it on my Sabbath. You see, I am a conscientious objector."

"Well, what do you know? We have us a CO." the sergeant said, plenty loud enough for everyone to hear. "I have no use for guys like you, now get to work," he demanded. The sergeant continued scolding Desmond for being a "mama's boy" and a coward. Desmond appealed to him again, telling the sergeant, that his beliefs prohibited him from doing work on the Lord's Day. "I'll work tomorrow, twice as hard," Desmond said to the now infuriated sergeant. "We need you today, not tomorrow!" the sergeant yelled. Frustrated at Desmond, the sergeant told him to get out of the barracks, before he threw him out.

Desmond, embarrassed at being scolded in front of the others, left the barracks and sat on the back steps. He pulled out his pocket Bible and began to read, hoping to find the encouragement he desperately needed at that moment. An officer, seeing Desmond sitting down reading, began yelling at him to get back inside. Desmond tried to explain that the sergeant had ordered him out, but the officer insisted that Desmond get back to work. The sight of Desmond coming in the door sent the sergeant into a rampage. "I thought I told you to get outside!" he yelled. When Desmond explained that an officer ordered him back in, the sergeant sat Desmond on the floor in a corner. It was demeaning to Desmond to be treated in such a juvenile way. The sergeant had purposefully embarrassed Desmond by kicking him out of the barracks, and now he was being treated like an unruly school child. The situation was made worse by the other recruits, who cursed at Desmond as they worked around him.

Three years had passed since that embarrassing incident, and now some of the same soldiers that had cursed Desmond and accused him of being a coward, watched as he bravely climbed to the top of the escarpment. When the three volunteers reached the top, the nets were raised and fastened into place. Then to the amazement of the soldiers below, Desmond stood upright so a photographer could snap a photo of him up on the ridge.

Since they had moved up from the beach-head to the base of the ridge, the 307th had been under almost continuous machine gun fire and mortar attacks. But amazingly, the entire time that Desmond was on top of the ridge, the firing had ceased. As Desmond stood there with his entire body silhouetted against the sky, he made a perfect target for one of the Japanese snipers in the area, but remarkably, not a single shot rang out. With the nets secure, the three volunteers scrambled back down the hill to rejoin their unit and await further orders.

On April 30, the orders to make the ascent up Hacksaw Ridge were received from Regimental Headquarters. The orders called for Companies A and B to simultaneously scale the ridge with Company A on the left flank and Company B on the right. Once on top, they were to secure the ridge and hold it until additional forces could be brought forward.

Desmond's platoon Commander, Lieutenant Gornto, called his men together to inform them that it was time to go up. Giving a short pep talk and relaying last minute instructions, Lieutenant Gornto finished by saying, "You have plenty of ammunition, now do your best men." Desmond had been to the top and had seen the terrain. He knew that, once up there, the men would be totally exposed to Japanese machine gun and mortar fire. Remembering the gruesome scene they encountered on the beach when they first landed, Desmond realized that there was a killing field that awaited them at the top of the ridge. As the Lieutenant completed his instructions, Desmond approached him with a request. "Lieutenant," Desmond said, "I believe prayer is the best life saver there is. The men should really pray before they go up." Remembering the sergeant back at Camp Lee, Desmond knew that he could very well be chastised for making such a request, especially at the onset of a battle; but unlike the sergeant who accused him of being a coward, Lieutenant Gornto immediately called to the men, "Fellows, gather round, Doss wants to pray for us."

Leading the men in prayer was not exactly what Desmond had in mind. He simply wanted the Lieutenant to remind the men that each of them should pray before they ascended the ridge. Desmond believed that many of these men would die that day, and he wanted to make sure they had an opportunity to make things right with God. However, like it or not, he had been handed the responsibility to pray, not only for himself, but for the safety of all the men in Company B. Unlike the incident at Camp Lee, or the many other times he experienced severe harassment since, there was no heckling and no cursing from the men. Without hesitation, they gathered together and bowed their heads.

"Dear Lord, Bless us today. Be with the Lieutenant and help him to give the right orders, for our lives are in his hands. Help each one of us to use safety precautions so that we might come back alive.

And, Lord, help all of us to make peace with Thee before we go up the net. Thank you, Amen."

Desmond's faith in God and his strong convictions were well known throughout the Seventy-Seventh Division. As a conscientious objector, Desmond refused to carry any type of weapon. Unlike others, who used the conscientious objector classification to avoid combat duty, Desmond fought hard throughout his service in the Army to remain a combat medic. On several occasions, officers in Desmond's chain of command tried to force Desmond to qualify with a rifle, but Desmond stood firm on his convictions and refused to carry or even hold a gun.

Throughout his training, Desmond had requested Saturday passes so he could attend church. Every time the Seventy-Seventh transferred to a new base, Desmond would find a local church where he would attend services. On the Saturdays he could not get a pass, he would stay in the barracks to read his Bible and pray, while the others went about their weekend duties. Desmond strongly believed in pulling his share of the work load, so he would work twice as hard, doing twice the amount of work, on Sundays. The other soldiers, who were irritated with Desmond's refusal to conform to their standards, would leave the dirtiest and most demeaning chores for him. On most any Sunday, Desmond could be found in the latrines cleaning toilets, in the mess hall washing dishes, or in the barracks scrubbing floors.

Every evening, Desmond would read his Bible and kneel by his bed to pray. During his prayer time, some of the soldiers in his barracks would entertain themselves by cursing at him, calling him a coward and throwing their boots at him. One soldier approached Desmond and told him that when they went into actual combat, Desmond was going to be the first person he shot. But through all the harassment and threats, Desmond remained steadfast with his prayers, his observance of the Lord's Day, and his commitment to never carry a gun, nor take a human life.

DOSS PRAYED

At the base of Hacksaw Ridge, with the prayers completed, Lieutenant Gornto gave the final order to move out and the men of Company B began climbing the cargo nets. Desmond assisted others as they struggled to get themselves and their equipment up the nets.

To their immediate left, the men of Company A had just reached the top of Hacksaw Ridge. As they scrambled over the ledge, the Japanese unleashed a hail storm of machine gun fire, immediately killing five soldiers. As Lieutenant Gornto and his men reached the top, the machine guns turned on them and they were immediately pinned down. Unable to find sufficient cover, Company A reported back to headquarters that both companies were under intense machine gun and mortar fire and were sustaining numerous casualties.

The machine gun fire was so intense that if a soldier stood up or even just raised his head, he was immediately shot. Hearing the reports of the situation on the top of the ridge, headquarters soon radioed Company B and asked for a casualty report. They were amazed when Desmond replied that Company B had no injuries or casualties. Company A had taken so many casualties, they could no longer stay in the fight; so headquarters ordered Company A to fall back and notified Company B that they would have to take the ridge alone. Lieutenant Gornto ordered the men to spread out along the top of the ridge. Staying low to the ground to lessen their profile, the men spread out to fill the void left by the retreating Company A.

The fierce firefight lasted throughout the entire day and, amazingly, Company B was able to hold on to a small portion of the plateau. Near the end of the day, Lieutenant Gornto ordered a final push forward and, after a fierce firefight, they successfully drove the Japanese off the top of the ridge. Once again the Americans held Hacksaw Ridge, but it would not last long.

When Lieutenant Gornto radioed the news of their victory back to headquarters, his superiors wanted a detailed account of their success. It was obvious that Company B had fought gallantly throughout the day, as Gornto reported they had knocked out eight or nine Japanese pill boxes (machine gun nests), and now controlled the entire plateau. However, the victory had come at a tremendous cost. Company A had been nearly annihilated, and Colonel Hamilton anxiously awaited the casualty report of Company B. However, the report they heard over the radio was unbelievable. Company B reported no casualties and only one minor injury. The sole injury was a cut to a soldier's hand, received when a rock fell on him while climbing back down the ridge.

The following day, headquarters requested a written report from Lieutenant Gornto describing how Company B was able to take and hold the ridge without a single casualty, while Company A, who was fighting right alongside them, was nearly annihilated. Gornto struggled with an answer, but he could not come up with a logical explanation for what appeared to be nothing short of a miracle. So Lieutenant Gornto sent his official report to headquarters with the simple explanation, "Doss prayed."

BACK AGAIN

The 307th was only able to hold the top of the ridge for a short while before the Japanese launched a counter attack and drove them back down the nets. On May 2, Company B was ordered to go back up the nets to take and hold Hacksaw Ridge. Doss wanted to pray for the men once again, but Lieutenant Gornto told him they did not have time, as the assault was already underway.

This time, the Japanese did not respond while they ascended the ridge. They waited until the entire company was on top before releasing an intense barrage of artillery, mortar, grenades and machine gun fire. Bullets filled the air like swarms of bees, and dozens of soldiers exposed on top of the ridge were immediately killed. Dozens more were wounded within just a few minutes of the fighting, and cries for medics came from all across the plateau.

Desmond, who was still at the base of the ridge, responded to the call for help and followed another medic up the cargo net. Once on top, the two medics found a severely wounded soldier lying near the edge. Both of his legs were blown off at the knees, and he had severe head and chest wounds. The first medic to reach him assessed his wounds and abandoned the unconscious soldier to go help others. Most medics operated under a system of treating the least wounded first so they did not expend time or medical supplies on those who did not have a chance. Desmond, however, operated under a totally different philosophy. He believed that if there is life, there is hope.

Desmond would never leave any soldier without treatment, regardless of the seriousness of their wounds. When Desmond saw the other medic leave the soldier without treating him, he ran to him and immediately began administering aid. After stopping the severe bleeding and bandaging his wounds, Desmond dragged the unconscious soldier off the escarpment and back to the aid station. Because of Desmond's commitment to saving every life he could, this soldier survived and lived to be seventy-two years old.

Once again, Company B was able to seize Hacksaw Ridge, but later that evening, the Japanese emerged from their tunnels and drove the Americans back down.

JUST ONE MORE

Operation Iceberg had been delayed long enough. Other units could not advance without the Seventy-Seventh Infantry Division securing Hacksaw Ridge and permanently holding it. Orders were sent from Headquarters on May 5, directing the entire Division to once again take the ridge, and this time hold it at all costs.

Colonel Hamilton, the Commander of the 307th, was again assigned to spearhead the attack. Colonel Hamilton briefed Captain Vernon and the other company commanders of their mission, and ordered them to move out right away.

May 5, 1945 was a Saturday and Desmond, observing his Sabbath, was back at the base of the ridge reading his Bible and praying. Captain Vernon approached Desmond and said, "Doss, would you mind going back up the escarpment today? You know you are the only medic we have left and we really need you." Desmond believed that it was alright for him to work on the Sabbath if he was saving life, so he agreed to go, but asked if he could finish his devotion and prayer before they moved out.

Captain Vernon realized that the entire Seventy-Seventh Division would move out all at once and that Desmond's request, if granted, would delay the entire operation. It was unlikely that such a request would be permitted, especially from a lowly private who had previously been labeled a trouble maker; but Desmond was the only medic available and they desperately needed him. Captain Vernon, considering the miracle that happened the last time Desmond prayed before they went into action, decided to take the request to the Regimental Commander, Colonel Hamilton. Colonel Hamilton had been with the 307th throughout their training, and was well acquainted with Private Desmond T. Doss, as their paths had crossed several times before.

During training back in the states, Colonel Hamilton had received numerous complaints about the medic in the 307th who not only refused to carry a weapon, but would not even touch one. Officers and NCOs had complained that Desmond was the weakest link of their unit and his uncompromising position was a distraction to the other soldiers. The complaints were not isolated to his status as a conscientious objector, but his weekly requests for passes to attend church were a source of frustration for the officers. Colonel Hamilton was concerned that Desmond was becoming a liability to the unit, and he determined that it was time to intervene.

There had been numerous attempts to break Desmond's will and shame him into carrying a weapon. Several officers had pointed out that other medics carried automatic pistols so they could defend themselves and the soldiers they were trying to help. They told Desmond that if he did not carry a gun, he was putting the lives of his fellow soldiers at greater risk. But Desmond's response to their criticisms was that he was serving in the Army to save life, not to take life.

In an effort to break Desmond and force him out of the Army, his superiors transferred him out of the Medical Corps and assigned him to a rifle company. Desmond's new Commander, Captain Cunningham, established a policy that every soldier had to qualify with the rifle before they would be given a pass or furlough. Knowing that Desmond requested weekly passes to attend church, Cunningham intended to make him choose which was more important, standing by his commitment to never touch a weapon, or going to church.

Desmond once went to Captain Cunningham to request a furlough so he could visit his brother, who was home from the Navy for a brief time, but Cunningham refused, stating that since he had not qualified with the rifle, his request was denied. Desmond was distraught and, without knowing where else to turn, he decided to take his appeal to the Colonel.

Desmond explained his situation to Colonel Hamilton, in hopes that he would respect his status as a conscientious objector and grant him a pass. But Hamilton had heard enough complaining about Doss, and felt that it was time to deal with this issue directly. "Doss, you come from Virginia, don't you?" Hamilton asked, "There are a lot of good men who have come from Virginia." Hamilton told Desmond about other Virginians who were dedicated to their Christian beliefs, and who were also great soldiers. Men like Stonewall Jackson and Robert E. Lee were Christian soldiers, who fought for their own religious liberties, but "Desmond," he said, "sounds like to me you are a goldbrick and a shirker." Hamilton told Desmond that because he would not carry a gun, he was letting others do his fighting for him and he did not deserve a furlough. Unmoved by the Colonel's attempts to shame him into compliance, as Desmond left the Colonel's office, he turned and said, "Colonel, I will be just as good of a soldier as you."

Two years after that encounter with Private Desmond T. Doss, Colonel Hamilton was ready to send his regiment back up Hacksaw Ridge. The entire invasion force was waiting on Colonel Hamilton's men to take and hold the ridge. But now he had a request to delay a major military action, from the same private who had caused him so much distress back in the states.

Whether it was because Desmond was the only medic available, or because of the miraculous victory a few days earlier when Desmond prayed for Company B, to the delight of the men of the 307th, Colonel Hamilton ordered the regiment to move out, but only after Private Desmond Doss had finished his devotion and prayers.

Captain Vernon relayed the message that the Division was waiting until Desmond was ready to go. About half an hour later, Desmond reported that he was ready, and the one hundred and fifty-five soldiers of Company B once again climbed the face of Hacksaw Ridge. Many of the men believed that they had already fought the toughest battle, and this was going to be nothing more than a mop-up operation. However, those thoughts were quickly dispelled, as the Japanese unleashed the most intense counter attack they had experienced on Okinawa.

When Company B reached the top of the escarpment, the Japanese began a furious barrage of mortars and artillery. Mortar shells exploded in clusters among the men, wounding all within range of the deadly shrapnel. Machine gun and rifle fire was so thick that rifles were cut to pieces and one soldier was even decapitated by Japanese machine gun rounds. Soldiers scrambled to find anything to use as cover from the continuous barrage of bullets. One soldier commented that as long as you heard the whizzing sound of the bullets, you knew you were still alive.

While this was the fiercest battle they had experienced at Hacksaw Ridge, Company B did not initially fall back; instead, they dug in and fought to maintain their ground. One soldier attempted to take out a Japanese machine gun nest by tossing a satchel of explosives into it. Quick thinking Japanese soldiers pulled the fuses out of the bags before they ignited. Two other soldiers hurled five gallon cans of gasoline into a Japanese foxhole, while another soldier followed by throwing a white phosphorus grenade to ignite the fuel. A tremendous explosion followed, with an even greater explosion further down the hillside. The blazing gasoline had ignited an ammunitions dump deep inside the Japanese tunnels.

As a result of the explosion, hundreds of Japanese emerged from their tunnels and charged with their bayonets drawn. Realizing they would not be able to hold the ridge, the order to withdraw was given, and the men of the Company B began scrambling back down the face of Hacksaw Ridge.

The Japanese continued their assault, even as the men began to fall back. Instead of retreating to safety, Desmond stayed on top to help several of the wounded back to the ledge and down the cargo nets. Finally, as Desmond was ready to descend the ridge, he noticed dozens of severely wounded soldiers scattered across the plateau. Desmond knew that if these men were left on top, they would surely die. The lucky ones would die from their wounds; the others would be tortured and eventually executed by Japanese night patrols. Desmond believed he had no choice but to save those that he could. Instead of following the others back down the cliff, he decided that he had to stay on top and help as many as possible.

Desmond ran to the soldier lying closest to the edge of the escarpment and began treating his wounds. Kneeling on the ground beside the soldier, without protective cover or even a weapon to fight back, Desmond was a prime target for Japanese snipers. Bullets flew by, as he desperately tried to save the life of this young man. Realizing that Desmond had remained on top, a soldier began yelling to him to get off the ridge. But Desmond continued his job of saving the man's life.

The soldier's wounds were very serious, and Desmond knew he had to get this man off the escarpment and back to the aid station quickly. The soldier, too wounded to move on his own, had to be carried back down, and Desmond would have to do this by himself. Desmond grabbed a litter, rolled the soldier on, and dragged him back to the edge of the ridge. With a rope he found lying near the edge, Desmond tied the soldier to the litter and lowered him down the face of the cliff. Several soldiers resting at the base of the cliff were surprised when they saw a man tied to a litter hanging over the edge. Desmond yelled for them to take the man to the aid station, "He's hurt bad," Desmond yelled. The soldiers untied the litter and hurried their wounded comrade to the aid station. Desmond turned and ran to another wounded soldier. Reaching the next one was even more dangerous, as he had to cross the wide open plateau. Keeping as low as he could to reduce his profile, Desmond ran as fast as he could. The Japanese, seeing Desmond running to the soldier's aid, began firing. "God," Desmond prayed as he ran, "please help me get another."

Desmond reached the soldier, assessed his wounds, and immediately began dragging him to the edge of the escarpment. This soldier was also too injured to climb down the cargo nets and Desmond did not have another litter. Desmond then remembered a knot he had accidentally discovered when he was learning to tie a bowline knot during mountain training in West Virginia. He quickly tied the double loop knot and placed a loop over each leg of the soldier. Desmond, who was already fatigued from the day's battle, needed something to assist in lowering this soldier down the cliff. When he finished securing the rope, he noticed a tree stump just at the edge of the escarpment. The stump was in a perfect position, so he wrapped the rope around it and slowly lowered the man to the waiting soldiers below. As soon as the soldiers untied the wounded man, Desmond pulled the rope back up to the top, prayed, "God, help me to get one more," and ran back into the field of fire to rescue another.

Desmond repeated this course of action throughout the night, bringing one soldier at a time to the edge of the escarpment, and lowering them to safety. All the time, Japanese snipers were trying to bring Desmond down, as he ran across the plateau. For five hours Desmond repeated the process; run to the wounded, treat him, drag him to the edge, lower him to safety, pray and start again. At one point, a soldier witnessed Desmond dragging a limp lifeless body across the plateau by the back of the shirt collar, while Japanese bullets whizzed around him. Another time he was seen helping two soldiers at once to the edge of the escarpment. Throughout the day, and without regard to the tremendous danger he was facing, Desmond continued rescuing his fellow soldiers from the top of Hacksaw Ridge.

Finally, after rescuing every soldier he could find, Desmond climbed down from Hacksaw Ridge. When he finally reached the aid station, he was soaked in blood and totally exhausted. Seeing the blood soaked uniform and assuming Desmond had been wounded, others came running to help him. When they reached him they were astonished to find that, although he was exposed to intense enemy gunfire for over five hours, he had not received a single wound.

Desmond was in rough condition. He was given a clean uniform and sent back to headquarters to clean up and rest. Desmond was in desperate need of rest, but instead of immediately going to sleep, he found a quiet place where he could read his Bible and pray.

Reports of Desmond's actions reached Division headquarters, and General A.D. Bruce paid a visit to the Seventy-Seventh Division to personally meet Private Doss. However, when the General arrived, Desmond could not be found. Again he was off alone reading his Bible and praying, and the two men never had a chance to meet. General Bruce believed Desmond's actions that day were worthy of the nation's highest honor, and wanted to recommend Desmond for the Medal of Honor. Desmond's valor and bravery were easily justifiable, but before he could submit the report, he had to know how many men Desmond had actually saved.

Officers from Division Headquarters were sent to interview Desmond and others who witnessed his heroic actions, to determine the number of men he rescued that day. Desmond's officers reported that one hundred and fifty-five men of Company B had climbed Hacksaw Ridge that morning and only fifty-five came down on their own. They accredited Desmond with single handedly saving one hundred men that day. Desmond, however, could not believe he had saved that many, and suggested that it could only have been about fifty. General Bruce had to have a number to submit with his recommendation, so Desmond and the officers compromised and officially reported that he saved seventy-five.

WOUNDED

Within a few days of Desmond's heroic actions, the 307th had finally secured the top of the escarpment and driven the Japanese further down the valley. With the escarpment now secured, the invasion of Okinawa could continue. As the 307th began pushing deeper into Okinawa, the Japanese continued their fierce resistance. The number of dead and wounded continued to increase, and Desmond continued his duty of tending to the injured, most often performing his duties while under enemy fire.

On May 21, two weeks after Desmond had rescued the men from Hacksaw Ridge, Company B was sent back into action. They were ordered to conduct a covert night mission to scout enemy locations. It was a dark, moonless night when Desmond moved out on foot with a small patrol force. About a half mile past the top of the escarpment, they walked into a Japanese ambush, and brutal hand-to-hand combat broke out. During this engagement, Desmond himself was severely wounded. Once again instinctively acting to save the lives of others, Desmond's legs were filled with shrapnel as he stepped onto a grenade to protect two other solders. As he was being evacuated, his arm was also hit and shattered by a Japanese sniper round; yet he continued to heroically tend to others who were injured along the way.

On May 23, 1945, with seventeen pieces of shrapnel removed from his legs, a badly fractured arm, and a bullet imbedded in his upper arm, Desmond Doss was headed back home to Virginia.

At a ceremony in Washington, D.C. on October 12, 1945, President Harry S. Truman awarded Desmond T. Doss the nation's highest award. He was the first conscientious objector ever to be awarded the Congressional Medal of Honor.

REFERENCES

"Bronze Star and Medal of Honor Charm." *National Medal of Honor Museum*. National Medal of Honor Museum of Military History. Web. 23 Jan. 2011.

The Conscientious Objector. Dir. Terry Benedict. Perf. Desmond T. Doss. Cinequest, 2004. DVD.

"Conscientious Objector, Medical-Aid Man, Awarded Medal of Honor." *The Advent Review and Herald* 1 Nov. 1945: 1-2. Web.

Doss, Frances M. *Desmond Doss: Conscientious Objector : the Story of an Unlikely Hero*. Nampa, ID: Pacific Pub. Association, 2005. Print.

Leckie, Robert. *Okinawa: the Last Battle of World War II*. New York, NY: Penguin, 1996. Print.

Lowe, H. W. "Conscientious Objector Awarded Medal of Honour." *British Advent Messenger* 28 Dec. 1945: 4. Web.

Sasser, Charles W. *God in the Foxhole: Inspiring True Stories of Miracles on the Battlefield*. New York: Threshold Editions, 2008. Print.

8

DORCHESTER HEIGHTS

General George Washington (1776)

"Arise, O Lord, and let our enemies be scattered! Let them flee before you!"
Numbers 10:34(NLT)

"Sir, they're moving!" General Washington's aid exclaimed as he swung open the flap of the commander's tent. Washington was quick to his feet as the young Lieutenant stepped inside to receive the orders he knew would follow. "Have all messengers assemble at the observation point, immediately!" Washington exclaimed as he donned his coat. "Yes Sir!" responded the Lieutenant. Expecting the British to attack his artillery emplacements on Dorchester Heights, Washington had ordered a continual observation of Boston, with instructions that he was to be notified immediately if there was any movement, especially around the harbor.

"Have Generals Greene and Knox been notified of this activity?" Washington asked as he stepped through the doorway. "No Sir, I reported directly to you," the Lieutenant replied as he followed Washington outside. "Very well," Washington replied, "have all staff officers assemble at the observation point at once. I will issue further orders from there." "Yes Sir!" the young man replied as he struck a sharp salute and quickly departed to fulfill his orders. Washington mounted his horse and, with an obvious sense of urgency, galloped toward the shores of Boston Harbor.

TAKING COMMAND

Nine months earlier, a rag-tag group of American volunteers had engaged the British on the outskirts of Boston, in an area known as Bunker Hill. These farmers, merchants, and businessmen had little to no military training. Their weapons were not military muskets, but common hunting rifles which were heavier and slower to load than the British "Brown Bess" muskets. Though their cannon were old and rusted, and gun powder was in short supply, this untrained group of colonists had bravely repulsed two British attacks and inflicted a staggering number of casualties on General Howe's highly trained *Redcoats*. Unable to withhold against a third British assault, the Americans were forced to retreat. These American patriots, who so bravely fought at Bunker Hill, possessed something that had proven to be mightier than British cannon, muskets, and bayonets; they had a commitment to the cause of liberty, and a strong belief in the protection of Divine providence.

With the British occupying the city of Boston, the Americans were forced to retreat across Boston Harbor, where they set up camp near the town of Cambridge. The Colonists had fought well at Bunker Hill and, although they had lost their first major engagement of the war for independence, their spirits were high and they were anxious to regroup and drive the British out of their city; however, they desperately needed supplies, training, and most of all leadership.

The news of Bunker Hill had not yet reached Philadelphia, where the Continental Congress was meeting, but Congress was already outraged by the British attacks at Lexington and Concord, and were eager to respond. Congress had been advised that an army of volunteers was assembled in Massachusetts, but they were mostly ordinary citizens, not trained soldiers. To engage in a war with the British, Congress needed to organize these volunteers into an Army; nonetheless, without a national treasury, they would have to raise money to acquire arms, ammunition and supplies. More importantly, Congress needed to appoint a Commander in Chief, who could take command and create an Army out of this untrained rabble. The man Congress selected would not only need to have military experience, he must also be well known and respected throughout the colonies.

On June 15, 1775, the Second Continental Congress unanimously selected George Washington of Virginia "to command all the Continental forces raised, or to be raised for the defense of American liberty." Washington, although highly honored to be considered for this command, responded to his nomination with reluctance, stating that he was deeply concerned that he did not possess the military skills or the experience required of such an important office. Although reluctant, he could not ignore his country's call for duty, so he accepted their unanimous nomination, and committed to Congress that he would "enter upon the momentous duty, and exert every power [he] possessed in their service, and for support of the glorious cause."

On June 20, Washington received orders from Congress to proceed without delay to the colony on Massachusetts Bay, and take charge of the Army of the united colonies. Washington and his newly appointed staff were in route to Massachusetts when the news of Bunker Hill reached them. The messenger was not aware of the outcome of the battle, but he was certain that it was a very bloody affair.

An official report of the engagement at Bunker Hill finally reached General Washington as he arrived in New York. A dispatch from General Gage, the acting commander of continental forces in Massachusetts, reported the Americans had successfully repulsed two attacks on their fortifications but, having exhausted their supply of powder and ammunition, they were unable to stop the third. Although this was the first combat for most, General Gage reported that "many stood and received wounds by swords and bayonets before they quitted their lines." These young, inexperienced and untrained soldiers were thrown into the worst of situations, but fought courageously. Unwilling to give up an inch of their homeland, they stood their ground even after their ammunition was gone. General Gage closed the letter by requesting that powder and ammunition be sent immediately, and that the new Commander in Chief, whoever the Congress had appointed, should arrive at once.

Washington arrived in Cambridge on a quiet Sunday afternoon in July of 1775. All along the journey from Philadelphia, Washington had been treated to welcoming parties, parades, dinners, and balls hosted in his honor. People would line the streets waving banners and cheering as Washington and his staff passed through the city. However, in Cambridge there were no welcoming committees, no city officials to greet them, no banners hung from windows, no bands played, nor citizens lined the streets. The General simply rode through the city, virtually unnoticed by anyone. He also entered the American encampments just as quietly as he entered Cambridge. Washington was not bothered by this seemingly cold reception; actually, he was uncomfortable with all the fanfare he had received along the journey. He realized that, as a Virginian, he would be considered a foreigner to this Army, which was primarily comprised of New Englanders. This alone would subject him to skepticism among the soldiers and fellow officers.

The following morning, the Army was assembled for inspection and a ceremonial parade was held in honor of their new commander. After reviewing the troops, Washington was briefed by General Gates and others about the number and location of American forces, the size and location of British forces, and the dismal status of supplies and ammunition. Washington, realizing there was a lot of work to be done, wasted no time in preparing these men for the battles that lay ahead.

Washington's immediate responsibility, according to his orders from Congress, was to prepare this Army to fight for the "glorious cause of liberty." On July 4, Washington issued his first official order as the Commander in Chief of the Continental Armies. Throughout the encampment, commanders called their units into formation and read the first official order from their new commander.

The General most earnestly requires and expects a due observance of those articles of war established for the government of the Army which forbid profane cursing, swearing and drunkenness. And in like manner he requires and expects of all officers and soldiers not engaged in actual duty, a punctual attendance of Divine services, to implore the blessing of Heaven upon the means used for our safety and defense.

This order revealed two very important beliefs that the General held throughout his life of public service. First and foremost, Washington believed in the power of prayer and God's Divine providence. During the French and Indian War, for instance, Washington often found himself in situations on the battlefield that should have resulted in his death; however, in each situation, Washington acknowledged that the "interposition of Divine providence" on his behalf, was the only explanation for his survival. Throughout the eight years of the war for independence, there would be numerous reported encounters of Washington, alone in his headquarters or out in the forest, praying for his men and their cause. Washington truly believed that, without God's assistance, the cause for which they were fighting would die on the battlefield.

Evidence of Washington's faith in God's intervention was recorded in a letter written to Brigadier General Thomas Nelson in 1778, "The hand of Providence has been so conspicuous in all this [the course of the war] that he must be worse than an infidel that lacks faith…" Even if this Army had a sufficient supply of weapons, ammunition and powder, they were fighting the greatest military force in the entire world and, without the assistance of Heaven, Washington knew there would be little chance of survival, much less victory.

Secondly, Washington believed, as his order indicated, that the spiritual condition of the soldier was more important than his combat skills or weapons. This belief was evident not only in his order to attend *Divine services* but, throughout the war, Washington continually encouraged his soldiers to conduct themselves as Christians. During their winter encampment at Valley Forge, where the harsh weather and lack of supplies threatened their very survival, Washington called on local clergy to augment his chaplains in conducting religious services for his men. Henry Muhlenberg, a Lutheran Pastor who lived near Valley Forge, wrote that "His Excellency General Washington rode around among his army yesterday and admonished each and every one to fear God, to put away the wickedness that has set in and become so general, and to practice the Christian virtues." Although his soldiers were freezing and starving, Washington believed that building spiritual strength was paramount to survival.

With the spiritual condition of the army attended to, Washington turned his attention toward physically preparing the men for battle. Throughout the summer and fall of 1775, the General and his staff focused on training, supplying and reorganizing this *rag-tag-rabble* into an army of American fighting men. While junior officers were training their men in the art of warfare, Washington and his staff were developing plans to drive the British out of Boston. Their attack had to be a swift and decisive blow, and Washington needed a plan that would not only force the British out of the city, but would convince them to abandon the fight and return to England. Washington believed that if properly planned and executed, this could be the final battle of the war and by autumn he would be on his way back home to Mount Vernon.

DORCHESTER HEIGHTS

While Washington rode his horse to the observation post located on a high hill overlooking Boston Harbor, his aide was advising staff officers that General Howe was making a move towards Dorchester Heights. The other officers hurried to meet Washington and to see if Howe was taking the bait and stepping into the trap they had set for him. The short ride gave Washington a chance to think about the battle that lay ahead and ponder the question that haunted his thoughts since being appointed to this post; did he posses the ability and experience to lead this Army?

At six foot three inches in height, Washington towered over most of the men in the Army. His hands were long and thick, and he walked with an air of authority. Washington's very appearance was intimidating to some, but his congeniality and strength of character caused even his harshest critics to treat him with the utmost respect. To the citizens of Virginia, Washington was a living legend, a hero, but to his fellow officers and several members of Congress, Washington's leadership was unproven, and many expressed their doubts about his ability. "This day," Washington must have thought as he rode, "will answer the question of my ability to every concerned party, both American and British."

Several of Washington's staff and subordinate field commanders were already assembled when the General arrived at the observation point. Most of them had telescopes to their eyes watching the British move troops and artillery. Washington brought his horse to a quick halt, dismounted, and removed his telescope to see what he prayed would be General Howe preparing for a full assault on Dorchester Heights. However, to the General's dismay, the British were not making a massive troop movement. General Howe was only moving artillery pieces and their crews onto "Boston Neck," a small peninsula on the southeastern tip of the city. On the streets of Boston, Washington could see hundreds of British soldiers and Bostonian citizens staring in amazement at the array of American artillery and defensive fortifications on Dorchester Heights, which had literally appeared overnight.

Dorchester Heights was a series of hills that ran just southeast of Boston. Both Generals, Howe and Washington, realized the strategic importance of this hilly peninsula that protruded into Boston Harbor. Cannon placed on the tops of the hills could easily strike targets inside the city as well as control the Harbor entrance, but neither army had previously attempted to occupy this strategic high ground. For the British to occupy the Heights, General Howe would have to pull forces out of Boston, leaving it vulnerable to a surprise attack. Washington, with his superior numbers, could easily spare the men to occupy the hills, but he did not possess artillery, and General Howe knew it. So throughout the winter of 1775, the most strategic point near Boston remained unoccupied by either Army.

SECRET MISSION

Washington had a very loyal and motivated command staff, but most of the officers were inexperienced. To compensate for their lack of formal military training, Washington encouraged his officers to study books and manuals on military tactics and warfare. Washington had noticed "a very fat but active young man," who seemed to always have a manual on artillery in his hands. Henry Knox's motivation, energy and determination impressed Washington and, considering the Continental Army lacked an artillery corps, he appointed the young bookseller from Massachusetts as his Commander of Artillery. With the self motivated Knox at the helm, Washington now had an artillery corps; unfortunately, it lacked an important resource- artillery.

In May of 1775, Fort Ticonderoga, a British garrison on the shores of Lake Champlain in northern New York, had been captured by a band of American militia. The *Green Mountain Boys* from Vermont, led by Ethan Allen, had joined forces with the Connecticut Militia, commanded by a young General named Benedict Arnold. Through an act of providence, they captured the entire fort with all its supplies, ammunition and armament intact, without firing a single shot. Their bounty included seventy artillery pieces with a full supply of gunpowder and ammunition.

Knox approached Washington with a bold plan. He proposed that, with winter soon setting in, he could take some men to Ticonderoga, disassemble the artillery and float it by barge across Lake George before it froze. They would then build sleds and, using oxen, drag the guns to Cambridge along the frozen roads and trails. The plan was thought to be hopeless by many of Washington's staff, but the General trusted Knox's ingenuity and determination, and approved. Knox immediately departed for New York with his corps, to ready their bounty for transport.

Four days later, Knox and his entourage arrived at Fort Ticonderoga and began disassembling the guns and loading them for their journey to Cambridge. Over the next two months, Knox and his men floated and drug the captured armament the three hundred miles to the anxiously waiting Washington. On January 24, 1776 Knox arrived with fifty nine artillery pieces, powder and ammunition. Although many of these cannon were antiquated, and others were covered with rust, they were functional and Washington now had an Artillery Corps, complete with artillery.

With the firepower he needed, Washington was ready to implement his plan to rid Boston of its British invaders. The first phase was to place his new Artillery Corps, with their recently acquired cannon, on Dorchester Heights. From this point, Washington could not only threaten the British positions inside Boston, but he could control the Harbor entrance. No British ship would attempt to enter the Harbor to bring Howe additional troops or supplies with Washington's cannon well within range.

Even with the ammunition and gun powder from Fort Ticonderoga, Washington could not engage in a sustained artillery battle; but having his artillery on the Heights would pose such a threat to General Howe, he would have to either attempt to drive the Americans from the Heights or evacuate Boston. Either action would suit Washington. If the British were to evacuate, he would have liberated Boston without a fight, but this was an unlikely scenario. Washington knew that by taking the high ground, he would be challenging General Howe, whose professional honor would prevent him from conceding. Washington's plan was to entice Howe to pull soldiers out of Boston to attack the artillery positions on the Heights, leaving Boston vulnerable. As soon as Howe began crossing the Harbor with his forces, Washington would float four thousand American troops down the Charles River and take the lightly defended city.

With increasing pressure from Congress for Washington to take some kind of action, the Army began preparing to occupy Dorchester Heights. Washington could not just go marching up the Heights, with artillery pieces in tow, during the middle of the day. If Howe suspected Washington had an Artillery Corps, he would most certainly attack immediately, in an attempt to stop them from gaining the high ground.

British spies sent word to General Howe of Washington's preparations to take the Heights, but Howe was unconcerned, stating "the Americans can only fight when they dig into the ground like moles, and the ground is too frozen to dig." Howe was correct; the ground was too frozen for the Americans to dig fortifications, so Washington had the men secretly building portable fortifications during the middle of the night. Frames called *fascines* were constructed out of sticks and limbs and, once in place, they would be filled with hay. Men worked relentlessly under the cover of darkness, night after night, assembling the cannon and building fortifications.

Then, on February 27 Washington issued an order that signaled to his Army that they would soon engage the British. Washington wrote, "As the season is now fast approaching, when every man must expect to be drawn into the field of action, it is highly necessary that he should prepare his mind, as well as everything necessary for it. It is a noble cause we are engaged in, it is the cause of virtue and, mankind, every temporal advantage and comfort to us, and our posterity, depends upon the vigor of our exertions." Washington's order emphasized the purpose of their fight, and spoke about the importance of "the favor of Divine providence." In addition to his order to prepare for battle, Washington called on nurses from nearby communities to be brought into the camp, and he ordered two thousand bandages to be made ready. It was clear to everyone that the battle of Boston would soon begin.

On the night of March 2, months of silence were finally broken as the American artillery, positioned on the opposite side of the Harbor from Dorchester Heights, began firing on Boston. This was not a full attack on the city, but simply a diversion to draw attention away from Dorchester Heights. To conserve gunpowder and ammunition, Washington ordered that only twenty five shots be fired. The British responded with their artillery, but their cannon balls fell short of the American lines and there were few injuries. For three nights, the same scenario ensued and, on the night of March 4, the American artillery began a full scale bombardment. Several artillery pieces fired at once, with a thunderous boom. They were followed by several more volleys and the British, realizing that this was an all out artillery assault, began focusing their attention on the American positions where the cannon fire was originating.

While blazing cannon balls flew back and forth across the sky leaving sparkling trails of light, thousands of Americans were quietly moving their artillery and portable fortifications towards Dorchester Heights, on the opposite side of the Harbor. Washington had ordered all soldiers to carry their muskets unloaded to ensure that one did not accidentally fire and reveal their clandestine activity. For hours, men pushed and pulled wagons loaded with the portable barricades, ammunition, gunpowder, and cannon across their lines and up Dorchester Heights. Washington watched and listened to the city below for any indication that the British had detected their movements, but all he could hear was the soft lapping of waves on the shore and the movement of men and horses behind him.

As the last fortifications were put into place, the sun began to rise above the horizon and the city below became alive with onlookers. As the word of what had mysteriously appeared on Dorchester Heights spread throughout the city, British officers hurried to the streets with their telescopes to see this unbelievable sight. The sight of the American artillery and the strange fortifications, which suddenly appeared overnight, caused wonder and fear among the British. One British engineer referred to their accomplishment as "an astonishing nights work" while another officer commented that the Americans must have employed a "genie from Aladdin's Lamp" to complete this task.

THE BATTLE OF BOSTON

With phase one complete, Washington only had to wait for Howe to load his troops into boats and cross the Channel. He ordered General Green to assemble his troops along the shores of the Charles River and wait for orders. Washington had just returned to his tent when his aid had stormed in with news that the British were moving. But as he arrived at the observation point, his officers had already advised him that Howe was only repositioning his artillery, not preparing an attack. Washington realized that Howe had not taken the bait that had been so carefully set. Instead of launching a ground assault, as Washington had predicted, he was preparing his artillery to fire at the American positions on the Heights. Washington lowered his telescope and turned to one of the messengers who had been standing quietly awaiting orders, "Notify General Knox to prepare for an artillery assault against his positions on Dorchester!" "Yes, Sir!" said the young messenger. He mounted his horse and took off.

Washington ordered positions on Dorchester to be strengthened, and several more artillery pieces were moved into place. Soldiers began filling barrels with rocks to be rolled down the hill on the advancing British, if they were to attack. Soon the silence was again broken, as British artillery let loose with their cannon; however, the balls fell short of the American positions and exploded harmlessly halfway up the hills. British engineers began digging the ground behind the cannon to lower the rear wheels and elevate the barrels. But the British were only wasting ammunition, as the Americans were too high for even their most powerful artillery. Shortly, the British attack was abandoned.

General Washington was preparing to return to his quarters when an officer shouted, "There's movement along the wharf, sir!" Washington, bringing his telescope to his eye, felt a sense of excitement. The British were bringing boats to the docks and assembling what appeared to be thousands of soldiers along the shore. "This is it," he thought, as his heart raced in anticipation. Soon the British began loading men into their boats, and rowing out into the Harbor. The next high tide would be about midnight and Washington knew the mud of low tide would keep the British from landing until then. Surely by dawn they would begin their attack on Dorchester, and Washington would begin his assault on Boston.

Washington sent orders to Generals Greene, Putnam, and Sullivan to load their boats and make ready to move toward Boston. He also sent word to General Thompson, who commanded the twenty-four hundred infantry positioned on Dorchester with General Knox's artillery, to prepare for a frontal assault. Things were beginning to go according to plan, and it appeared to Washington that soon the British would be on their way back to England. However, the same Divine providence that Washington so dearly depended on for victory, would soon intervene to stop his plans and save his Army from annihilation.

Washington's intelligence had grossly miscalculated the strength of the British. Boston was more heavily defended than Washington had anticipated, and his men were unknowingly headed into a potential massacre by an overwhelming British force still guarding Boston. But once again, as so many times in Washington's life, Providence intervened. Just as Washington was ready to order the men to move down the Charles River toward Boston, the sky turned dark and a storm of incredible proportions blew furiously into the Harbor. Huge waves churned, making the river impassable. One British soldier described the storm as having winds "more violent than anything I have ever heard." Washington was clearly distressed by this unfortunate turn of events, but he believed that Providence "for some wise purpose," had altered his plan. Washington reluctantly recalled his men from the Charles River and canceled the invasion they had planned for so long. Fortunately, the storm also forced General Howe to recall his troops, which were preparing to attack the Americans on Dorchester Heights.

The storm subsided by dawn, and the light from the morning sun revealed that all was just as it had been the day before. The

British were still in Boston and the American artillery was still threatening from the top of Dorchester Heights. Through nothing short of a miracle, General Howe ordered an immediate evacuation of Boston, and soon the sails of British ships were seen entering the Harbor to evacuate the British soldiers. As soon as the British ships set sail, the Americans began moving in to secure the city. Washington could not allow the entire Army to move down into Boston, due to a Small Pox epidemic, so he sent word for his commanders to select men who had already had the Pox to form an advance guard which would march into Boston. Fortunately, Washington had contracted the disease earlier in life and was now immune.

Rumor soon spread among the citizens that Washington would lead the Army's grand march into Boston. Cheering bands of citizens began gathering along the streets, as the sounds of the American fifes and drums could be heard in the distance. Children climbed up on father's shoulders to get a better view of their Army, as it triumphantly marched into town. Bostonians were finally liberated, thanks to their new General, who was no longer viewed as a foreigner, but a hero. Hundreds of citizens, eager to catch a glimpse of General Washington, crowded along the streets but, to their disappointment, Washington was not leading the victory march into Boston, nor was he seen among the other officers and soldiers. Concerned about their Commander, people began asking those marching by, "Where is Washington?"

While the victorious American army was marching through the streets of Boston, back at the American Camp, a chaplain was holding church services for those who had stayed behind. The sermon delivered on this momentous occasion was from the text of Exodus Chapter 14, verse 25 "The Egyptians said, let us flee from the face of Israel; for the Lord fighteth for them against the Egyptians." While his men enjoyed the pomp and praise of the citizens of Boston, Washington had purposefully stayed behind. In accordance with his own orders, the General was taking the opportunity to attend "Divine services," where he once again thanked God for His almighty protection.

REFERENCES

Clinton, George. *Public Papers of George Clinton*. Albany: Quayle, 1901. Print.

Hamilton, W. J. *Ethan Allen's Rifles, Or, The Green-Mountain Boys*. New York: Beadle and Adams, 1873. Print.

Flexner, James Thomas. *George Washington: the Forge of Experience, 1732-1775*. Boston: Little, Brown, 1965. Print.

Flexner, James Thomas. *George Washington in the American Revolution: (1775-1783)*. Boston (Mass.): Little Brown, 1968. Print.

Marshall, Peter, and David Manuel. *The Light and the Glory*. Old Tappan, NJ: Revell, 1977. Print

Silvey, Anita, and Wendell Minor. *Henry Knox: Bookseller, Soldier, Patriot*. Boston [Mass.: Clarion, 2010. Print.

Thacher, James. *Military Journal of the American Revolution*. [New York]: New York Times, 1969. Print.

9

A TIME TO FIGHT

Reverend John Peter Gabriel Muhlenberg (1776)

"To every thing there is a season, and a time to every purpose under the heaven:... A time of war, and a time of peace"
Ecclesiastes 3:1 ,8

Sunday mornings were always so peaceful, especially during the predawn hours of winter, when Reverend Muhlenberg would walk the streets of Woodstock, Virginia on his way to church. Early in the morning, most of the houses along the way were still dark, with the residents enjoying the warmth of their beds. Occasionally, the flickering light of a lantern could be seen through a window as an early riser prepared their home for the Lord's Day. However, once the sun's light broke on the horizon, the serenity of night would give way to the sights and sounds of an eighteenth century American colony, with dogs barking, horses and carriages rumbling down the street, and the ringing of church bells. But at this early morning hour, not only was there peace from the daily activity of life, Reverend Muhlenberg felt it was also as if the evils of the world all ceased when the town was at rest.

This Sunday morning in early January, 1776 started like so many others for Reverend John Peter Gabriel Muhlenberg, the pastor of the Woodstock Lutheran Church. It was only a few days earlier that the town of Woodstock had welcomed in the New Year and the members of his church prayed that this year would be better than the previous. The year 1775 had been a tumultuous one for the northeastern American colonies, and Virginia was now becoming more involved in the growing conflict.

For several years, tensions between America and England had been escalating as the King tightened his grip on the colonies. Protests, staged by patriots demanding liberty and religious freedom, resulted in more retribution from the King. In response to the growing anti-British sentiment, King George sent more soldiers to keep the colonists in line; however, this incited additional protests and more civil unrest. Then in April of 1775, tensions reached the breaking point when British soldiers marched on the towns of Lexington and Concord in the Massachusetts Colony. There they were met by bands of American volunteers, known as minutemen, and when the two forces collided, muskets were fired, men fell, and the war for American independence began.

Soon after the engagements at Lexington and Concord, the British attacked the colonist's positions on Breeds and Bunker Hills on the outskirts of Boston. An untrained army of American volunteers put up a valiant fight but, in the end, they were forced to retreat after exhausting their limited supplies of gunpowder and ammunition. They withdrew their remaining forces and repositioned across Boston Harbor near the town of Cambridge. As soon as they set up camp, a request was sent to Philadelphia, where the Continental Congress was meeting. The volunteers were anxious to drive the British out of Boston, but their Army urgently needed training, supplies and most of all a General to lead them. To provide the needed ammunition and supplies, Congress would have to raise the money, since there was no money in a national treasury. In response to their request for leadership, Congress appointed one of their own delegates, George Washington of Virginia, to be the Commander in Chief of the American colonial forces.

Reverend Muhlenberg had met George Washington several years earlier, and the two men established a friendship and frequently wrote to one another. On this morning, as Muhlenberg made his way through the snow covered streets of Woodstock, Virginia to prepare for another Sunday morning sermon, Washington was in Cambridge preparing to invade Boston.

A few months earlier, Washington sent Congress a letter requesting all colonies to recruit volunteers to join the fight against tyranny. Congress complied and forwarded the call to arms to each colony's legislature. Throughout the fall and winter of 1775, Washington received a steady stream of new volunteers from several colonies, but most came from those that surrounded Massachusetts. With the battle so far away, there had only been a few Virginians willing to take up arms and join Washington. But Muhlenberg knew that, even though the battles were being fought in colonies further north, unless Washington was successful in defeating the British at Boston, the war would inevitably come to Virginia. All indications were that the peace Virginia currently enjoyed would soon be gone, just as the peace of this morning would soon change with the dawning of the day. The bright side of all this turmoil, to the Reverend, was the increase in church attendance. Muhlenberg was privileged to speak to a full church almost every Sunday, and today Reverend Muhlenberg hoped for a capacity crowd.

Brilliant beams of sunlight were just beginning to break the horizon when Reverend Muhlenberg finally arrived at the Lutheran Church. It was still several hours before the congregation would arrive for the service, but Muhlenberg needed this time to pray and prepare his message. This sermon, like so many others he had delivered, would tread on what some ministers considered forbidden territory; politics. More than once, Muhlenberg had been criticized by fellow ministers, and some of his own congregation, for using the pulpit to encourage support for independence. He was accused of heresy, treason and using his position to incite rebellion against the King of England. Muhlenberg believed his actions were patriotic, not treasonous, and God himself had given him the inspiration to preach the message of freedom. He believed, as another highly respected Virginian, Thomas Jefferson, stated that "rebellion against tyranny was obedience to God," and Muhlenberg never backed down from his convictions.

The Reverend's political involvement was well known to everyone in Woodstock. Not only was he a respected minister, he had also served as a delegate in the Virginia House of Burgess and was appointed by Dunmore County as the Chairman of the Committee on Public Safety. The more he became involved in political interests, the more criticism he received from his superiors in the Lutheran Church. To a fellow minister that had criticized him for his involvement in political and military affairs, Reverend Muhlenberg wrote, "I am a clergyman, it is true, but I am a member of society as well as the poorest layman, and my liberty is as dear to me as to any man. Shall I then sit still, and enjoy myself at home, when the best blood of the continent is spilling? Heaven forbid it! … I am called by my country to its defense. The cause is just and noble. …I am convinced it is my duty so to do, a duty I owe to my God and to my country."

Some of Muhlenberg's congregation believed his preaching was too controversial for a minister of the gospel, but others were inspired by his fiery and often emotional messages. Since receiving Washington's call for recruits from the Virginia legislature, a few men from his congregation had left Woodstock to join the cause, and others had vocally supported the idea of independence; but with the war so far away, only a few were willing to leave their homes and families to fight the British.

Muhlenberg wanted to help Washington with recruiting. He believed that, with enough volunteers, Washington could not only drive the British out of Boston but, with a decisive victory, he could break their will to continue this war. It was quite possible the war could end before it ever reached Virginia, but Washington needed men, and Muhlenberg was driven to help recruit them.

Although he believed his sermons may have helped inspire those who had joined the cause, Muhlenberg began wondering if his preaching was enough. The Bible calls us to be "doers" not just "hearers" of the word, he often told others, and he believed that God was calling him to do more for the cause in which he so strongly believed.

Since childhood, it had been expected that Muhlenberg would follow in the footsteps of his ancestors, choosing the ministry as his profession. Even his given name was suited for a great messenger of Christ. His parents named him John Peter Gabriel, in honor of three great messengers from the Bible. His first name, John, was in honor of *John the Baptist,* who preceded Christ and announced the message that a savior would soon come. John the Baptist was by all accounts the first minister of Jesus Christ. This name was very fitting for the Reverend, as the Biblical John's preaching was often controversial and treaded on subjects that stirred deep emotion.

Muhlenberg's second name, Peter, was in honor of the *Apostle Peter,* who is credited as being the founder of the Christian Church. Peter's name was given to him by Jesus, who said that Peter would be the rock on which the church was built. After Christ's resurrection, Peter, *the rock,* continued preaching the gospel to the Jews. Muhlenberg's third name honored *Gabriel,* the messenger or announcing angel of God. Gabriel visited the virgin Mary and informed her she would miraculously bear a child, conceived of the Holy Spirit.

At this time, Reverend John Peter Gabriel Muhlenberg was fulfilling what his parents believed to be his destiny; a messenger of the gospel of Christ. But he felt a growing sense that God was calling him to do more than just preach the gospel. He still believed in this calling and continued to spread the message of Christ, but God had something more in store for him, and he was determined to follow God's calling.

Muhlenberg opened the door to a small room, which served as his pastoral study. He lit a lantern and hung his clerical robe on a hook beside the door to the sanctuary. He sat down at a small wooden desk, opened his Bible to the book of Ecclesiastes, and began to read. As he delved deeper into the scriptures, time seemed to pass quickly, and before long he could hear the first comers of his congregation gathering in the sanctuary. He checked the time on his watch, then continued preparing his mind and spirit for the morning's sermon, which he prayed would be more inspirational than any message he had ever delivered.

A rumor had circulated through the town that this may be Muhlenberg's last sermon. This had attracted a larger than normal crowd, and the church pews were quickly filling. As the voices and commotion from the sanctuary grew louder, Reverend Muhlenberg checked the time again and saw that it was time to start the service. Closing his Bible, he stood up from the desk and carefully pulled his clerical robe over his clothing. Checking to be sure his clothes were fully covered by the robe, he quietly entered the sanctuary. When Muhlenberg entered, all the commotion ceased and a hush fell over the congregation. With his Bible in hand, he slowly ascended the steps to the pulpit to give what was, indeed, going to be his last sermon to the people of Woodstock, Virginia.

He opened his Bible and began to read from the Old Testament book of Ecclesiastes, Chapter three verses one through eight. "To everything there is a season, and a time to every purpose under heaven," he started.

"A time to be born, and a time to die; a time to plant and a time to pluck up that which is planted; A time to kill, and a time to heal; a time to break down, and a time to build up; A time to weep, and a time to laugh; a time to mourn, and a time to dance; A time to cast

away stones, and a time to gather stones together; a time to embrace,
and a time to refrain from embracing; A time to get, and a time to
lose; a time to keep, and a time to cast away; A time to rend, and a
time to sew;"

For an hour and a half, he preached about duty, responsibility and obedience to God's calling. He then read, "There is a time to keep silence and a time to speak." While others remained silent, especially in church, about the tyranny the colonies were under, he determined now was the time to speak. He had been warned numerous times to keep quiet about his support of independence, but even the scriptures were proclaiming that there is a time to speak. His eyes scanned the congregation, and it was obvious that, whether or not they agreed, all eyes were fixed upon him. He was not sure if he was inspiring them, but he knew they were all listening.

With the congregation entranced by his fiery oration, he once again returned to the scriptures and read, "There is a time to love, and a time to hate, a time of war, and a time of peace." Upon reading that passage, Muhlenberg paused and stood quietly looking across the large congregation. He placed his Bible on the pulpit, signifying that he was departing from his prepared sermon, and said, "In the language of the Holy Writ, we see there is a time for all things. But there is also a time to preach and a time to pray, but the time for me to preach has passed away." He stepped back from the pulpit and concluded his sermon by saying, "There is also a time to fight, and that time has now come." Then, to the surprise of the congregation, he slowly removed his clerical robe, revealing the uniform of a Colonel in the Continental Army.

As church members gasped in astonishment, he descended the pulpit. Instead of returning to his study, he marched down the center aisle to the back of the sanctuary. Upon reaching the back of the church, he opened the doors where there stood in the street a drummer, in full military uniform, who began playing the *Call to Recruits*. Muhlenberg turned to his congregation and said, "Who will join me in the fight for liberty?" By the end of that cold January day, over three hundred men responded to Reverend Muhlenberg's call and the Eighth Virginia Regiment was established. With their new commander and former pastor in charge, they immediately marched off to South Carolina to assist in the relief of Charleston.

John Peter Gabriel Muhlenberg never officially returned to the pulpit after his dramatic resignation, but he continued serving God through an illustrious service to his country.

During the winter of 1777, the recently promoted General Muhlenberg spent the harsh winter with George Washington and his Army at Valley Forge. Washington relied heavily upon his chaplains and ministers, including General Muhlenberg, to boost the morale of the freezing and starving men. Ironically, a nearby resident of Valley Forge, who was also a Lutheran minister, regularly visited General Washington at the camp. This minister often spoke of how General Washington rode around the camp encouraging his soldiers to repent and pray. This minister was General Muhlenberg's father, Henry Melchoir Muhlenberg, who strongly opposed his son's abrupt abandonment of the ministry to join the Continental Army. However, Reverend Henry Muhlenberg must have been proud to know that his son was there, with General Washington, to minister to the men of the Colonial Army during the darkest hours of the American Revolution.

John Peter Gabriel Muhlenberg continued his service with General Washington through the end of the Revolutionary War. After the war, he served as Vice President of Pennsylvania under Benjamin Franklin and was a delegate to the Constitutional Convention in 1787. He later served in the U.S. Congress and the U.S. Senate.

Today, in the United States Capitol building, stands a statue of a minister removing his clerical robe. Tourists taken into this hall often walk by this statue never knowing the significance of his story. Reverend John Peter Gabriel Muhlenberg listened to God's call on his life and this *Fighting Parson*, as he was nick-named, is considered to be one of the heroes of the Revolution.

REFERENCES

Flexner, James Thomas. *George Washington: the Forge of Experience, 1732-1775.* Boston: Little, Brown, 1965. Print.

Flexner, James Thomas. *George Washington in the American Revolution: (1775-1783).* Boston (Mass.): Little Brown, 1968. Print.

Marshall, Peter, and David Manuel. *The Light and the Glory.* Old Tappan, NJ: Revell, 1977. Print

Marshall, Peter, and David Manuel. *The Glory of America.* Bloomington, MN: Garborg's Heart 'N Home, Inc., 1991. Print

Muhlenburg, Henry A. *The Life of Major-General Peter Muhlenburg of the Revolutionary Army.* Philadelphia: Carey and Hart, 1849

Thacher, James. *Military Journal of the American Revolution.* [New York]: New York Times, 1969. Print.

10

LEFT IN THE HANDS OF GOD

General Dwight D. Eisenhower (1943)

"The Lord hath heard my supplication; The Lord will receive my prayer. Let all mine enemies be ashamed and greatly troubled: let them return and be ashamed suddenly."
Psalm 6:9-10

Surrounded by several of his staff officers, General Dwight D. Eisenhower climbed to the top of a hill on the island of Malta. Although the main element of *Operation Husky* had set sail the previous day, the advance airborne units, who would soon be parachuting behind enemy lines, were about to depart and Eisenhower felt he needed to be there when they left. Reaching the summit, he walked to the edge of a cliff and stared out into the ocean. It was the evening of July 9, 1943 and somewhere beyond the horizon the massive armada of British and American warships fought through powerful winds, driving rain and huge swells brought on by a violent storm. Waves were so large they crashed over the ships bows. General George Patton, who was aboard the *USS Ancon*, knelt down in his quarters and prayed, as the waves unmercifully slammed into the ship's hull.

The nearly three thousand ships, loaded with American and British soldiers, ammunition and supplies, would soon be nearing the coast of Sicily. If the storm subsided, the thousands of invasion forces would leave the safety of the ships just before dawn and, while still under the cover of darkness, storm the rocky shores of Sicily. The uncertainty of what may await these brave men tore at the conscience of Eisenhower and, although he would remain on Malta during the initial phase of the operation, his mind and spirit were with his men.

As the supreme commander of this operation, Eisenhower was fully liable for its success or failure, and his decision to proceed while a massive storm was bearing down on the armada now weighed heavily on the General. The storm was not the only factor that made the success of this operation doubtful; there were other, more serious, factors that also plagued the General's thoughts. Would German artillery and machine guns be waiting to cut down the soldiers as they landed on the shore? Did Hitler fall for the deception they planted, and relocate the majority of his forces to the northern end of the island? Would the airborne troops hit their landing zones undetected and be in place before the infantry hit the beaches? Even though the finest strategists in both the British and American Armies had planned the invasion, Eisenhower knew that too many things could go awry and the mission could end in disaster for both nations. These pressures and uncertainties so plagued Eisenhower's thoughts, he was quoted as saying that they made his stomach feel as if it were "a clenched fist."

Operation Husky was the largest, best equipped and best trained invasion force the world had ever seen; but even that did not ease Eisenhower's mind. For months, strategists developed battle plans which were rehearsed, tweaked and rehearsed again. Soldiers practiced assault landings from newly developed landing craft, while paratroopers filled the skies, honing their airborne skills.

Unlike other invasions, Eisenhower did not use the Air Corps to conduct pre-invasion attacks. Although these bombing runs could take out some of the enemy's key defenses, Eisenhower wanted the explosions of Naval artillery shells and the sight of a half-million armed Allied soldiers storming the shores, to be the first indication of where the invasion would occur. Maintaining the secrecy of the invasion's location was his highest priority. If the Germans anticipated the spot on Sicily where they would strike, *Operation Husky* could be the bloodiest day in the history of the U.S. military.

COMMAND DECISION

Due to the storm that suddenly appeared in the Mediterranean Sea, Eisenhower's staff urged him to postpone the invasion and call back the forces. Eisenhower struggled with whether to break radio silence and recall the largest invasion force in the history of the world. The General was pressured from all sides to make his decision. A message was sent to Eisenhower from General George, C. Marshall, the U.S. Army's Chief of Staff in Washington D.C., which bluntly asked, "Is Husky on or off?"

Trusting the storm would subside, Eisenhower responded, "The operation will proceed as scheduled."

With this command decision, the invasion, these men, and the outcome of the mission, were now fully his responsibility and, right or wrong, it was a decision he would have to live with.

As he stood gazing into the darkness, Eisenhower could hear the roar of the Air Corps' transport planes overhead, as they carried the airborne soldiers to their nighttime landing zones. Though he looked towards the sky, through the darkness and the falling rain, he could only hear the drone of their engines as they climbed into the night. In just a short time, these men would parachute into hostile enemy territory. They would be the first on the island, the first in battle, and if things did not go as planned, they would be the first to die. Eisenhower confessed, "…there is no denying that I feel the strain."

The preparations for this day began six months earlier, as brutal fighting between Allied forces and the German Army in Africa was drawing to a close. In January, 1943 President Franklin Roosevelt and British Prime Minister Winston Churchill met in Casablanca to determine the Allies' next move. It was obvious their next operation would have to be an invasion of Italy, so the Casablanca conference was primarily to determine exactly where to strike. Since the Allies controlled the small island of Malta, located just sixty miles south of Sicily, it would be an ideal location from which to launch the invasion. With only a few miles of the Mediterranean separating the two islands, the southern tip of Sicily was the obvious place for the Allies to land. In fact, it was so obvious, Winston Churchill affirmed, "Everyone but a bloody fool would know it's Sicily." Surely the Germans would realize the strategic advantage of striking the southern shores of Sicily, and Hitler would have ample time to relocate his forces to thwart the invasion.

As planning for *Operation Husky* began, Eisenhower knew the rough terrain of Sicily favored the defenders, and he knew the fighting would be brutal, especially if the Germans were able to predict when and where the invasion would take place. But Sicily had to be taken, as it was a strategic point for controlling shipping lanes into the Mediterranean, and it would be a gateway for the Allies to push the Nazis out of Italy.

Invading a well defended island would require a massive, well trained and well equipped force. The Army and Navy would need an unprecedented amount of supplies and equipment, the majority of which would have to be shipped from the United States and staged in England, before being transferred to Malta. It would be nearly impossible to conceal the buildup of arms and supplies from German intelligence, which was already closely monitoring the Allies' shipping activity. Eisenhower and his commanders clearly understood that Germany would undoubtedly anticipate an invasion of Sicily and, by monitoring shipping and air cargo activity into Malta, they would easily be able to predict when the attack would occur. The only unknown factor for the Germans would be where on Sicily the Allies would strike. With the location being the only strategic advantage, Eisenhower kept it a closely guarded secret.

A Significant Discovery

During the early stages of World War II, Germany established an extensive espionage network throughout Europe. Numerous undercover agents worked, lived and played alongside peaceful citizens in England. They were some of the best intelligence operatives in the world and when Hitler needed information, they were very good at providing it.

As the massive buildup of arms and supplies began arriving in Malta, Hitler activated his spy network with orders to gain any and all intelligence that would reveal where the Allies would strike. Agents throughout England, using covert radio receivers, intercepted communications between Allied command units, watched for a buildup of supplies at logistics depots, and reported all shipping activity.

It was clear that an invasion was eminent, but German intelligence had not reported anything that indicated where the invasion would take place. Hitler had always suspected the Allies would land somewhere along the Southern tip of Sicily, but Winston Churchill had also publicly supported an invasion of the "Soft Underbelly of Europe," which was northern Sicily or southern Italy. Unsure of where to concentrate his forces, Hitler ordered intelligence operations to be intensified, hoping to procure this vital information.

For months German intelligence came up empty handed, but Hitler had to take action. Just as he was preparing to reinforce Sicily's southern coast, German authorities reported that they had made a significant find. A Spanish fisherman had recovered the body of a British officer floating in the Atlantic Ocean, off the coast of Spain. The deceased officer was wearing a life vest, and a locked briefcase was chained to his waist. Inside the case, German officers found documents that would ultimately affect the outcome of the invasion.

The British officer's body was immediately handed over to German intelligence, which soon identified it as that of Major William Martin of the British Royal Marines. To ensure the credibility of the information found on Major Martin, they had to first verify his identity. Intelligence operatives immediately began investigating the life of Major William Martin.

Intercepting Allied radio communications, agents confirmed that a plane was reported missing in route from England to the Allied Headquarters in North Africa. A short time later, the name of Major William Martin appeared on a casualty list printed in a London newspaper.

The investigation was thorough and uncovered much of Major Martin's official and personal life. Born in Candif, Whales in 1907, the British officer was currently assigned to the Combined Operations Headquarters in England. Through analyzing photographs and personal letters found on his body, it was discovered he had a fiancé named Pam. Martin also appeared to be rather careless; his bank records showed that his account was often overdrawn, and the temporary military identification card he was carrying was issued to replace one he had recently lost.

Everything seemed to confirm the credibility of their dead informant, and the reliability of the information he was carrying. Inside the sealed briefcase were letters from two British commanders, that referred to the Sicily invasion as a feint. The real invasion would be on the island of Greece and northern Sicily. Finally, the Germans had the break they were looking for, and Hitler ordered one Panzer Tank division from France, two from Russia, and an additional Waffen SS brigade to reinforce existing forces on the northern tip of Sicily.

THE INVASION

Still surrounded by his senior officers, Eisenhower remained quiet as he stood atop the mountain listening to the planes heading northward towards Sicily. In Eisenhower's eyes, these were not just weapons of war. These were men with families; his countrymen and his allies. They were more than just soldiers, sailors and airmen; they were his men and, as their commander, they were his responsibility and he desperately desired to be with them. When he could no longer hear the planes, and without speaking, Eisenhower solemnly raised his hand and saluted his men. Lowering his hand, he bowed his head and began to pray for these brave defenders of freedom. Completing his prayer, he lifted his head and turned to face the small crowd of officers, and said resolutely, "There comes a time when you've used your brains, your training, your technical skill, and the die is cast and the events are in the hands of God, and there you have to leave them." Moved with great emotion, and without speaking another word, Eisenhower descended the mountain to wait for reports from Sicily.

Just before dawn on July 10, 1943 the assault phase of *Operation Husky* began, as the door of first amphibious landing craft lowered, and the troops stormed the beaches on the southern tip of Sicily. Expecting fierce resistance, soldiers clambered along the shore looking for cover. But the defense was amazingly light and, within a short time, the Italian soldiers defending the coastline surrendered. Encountering mostly Italian forces, Eisenhower realized they had caught the Germans by surprise. Based on the information found on Major Martin, Hitler had concentrated his forces on the northern shores of Sicily, over eighty miles from where the Allies had landed. General Montgomery met such light resistance, he ordered the Eighth Army to push inland toward Catania without delay.

Realizing the deception, Hitler immediately moved his forces southward to intercept the Americans and British. America's First Infantry Division, under the command of General George Patton's Seventh Army, met strong resistance from a German division sent to halt their advance. But within a couple of days of fierce fighting, the Americans broke through and began moving further inland. By August 17, General Patton's Seventh Army and British Field Marshall Montgomery's Eight Army had completely taken the island of Sicily.

The Man Who Never Was

Fortunately for Eisenhower, Hitler had fallen for one of the greatest deceptions in military history. Not only were the documents recovered by the Germans falsified, but Major William Martin never existed. The entire life of William Martin had been completely manufactured by British intelligence, in a rather macabre scheme, known as *Operation Mincemeat*. His birth records, lodge memberships, and even his overdrawn bank account, were set up by British intelligence. The letters from his fiancé, Pam, were actually written by a secretary at intelligence headquarters, who also provided a picture of herself to be placed in Martin's wallet. Knowing German intelligence was active in London, British intelligence crafted false reports of a missing plane, and had Martin's name included in the newspaper's casualty report. Every aspect of Major Martin's life had been carefully constructed by British intelligence as a grand deception.

The body found floating in the Atlantic was that of a man acquired from a British morgue, who had died of pneumonia. British intelligence contacted the family of the deceased and requested the body, so it could be used for a worthy cause. With the promise that their loved one would receive a proper burial, the family agreed under one condition; the true identity of the young man must never be revealed.

The body was put into a British uniform, given the false documents, frozen in dry ice, and loaded aboard the British Submarine, HMS Seraph, which immediately headed for the coast of Spain. After a brief ceremony and a prayer, led by the submarine's commander, it was placed into the ocean. The *Seraph* dove to periscope level and waited throughout the night, until a Spanish fishing boat recovered the body of the fictitious Major William Martin.

The true identity of Major William Martin may never be known, though some amateur historians claim to have uncovered the mystery. After the investigation, Martin's body was laid to rest by the Spanish government in the Cemetery of Solitude in Huelva. The grave is marked by a plain white marble tombstone bearing the inscription, "William Martin. Born 1907. Died 24th April 1943. Beloved son of John Glyndwr Martin and the late Antonia Martin of Candif, Wales." In the center of the stone, inscribed in Latin, is the phrase "It is sweet and fitting to die for one's country." Regardless of William Martin's true identity in life, in death he played a crucial role in the victory at Sicily, saving the lives of thousands of Allied soldiers.

The successful invasion of Sicily was the beginning of the end for the German's occupation of Europe. Modern historians credit the success of the Sicily campaign to the extensive planning and training of the Allied Armies, as well as the deception created by *Operation Mincemeat*; however, in Eisenhower's own words, spoken from a mountain top on the tiny island of Malta, *Operation Husky* was ultimately left "in the hands of God."

REFERENCES

D'Este, Carlo. *Eisenhower: a Soldier's Life.* New York: Henry Holt &, 2002. Print.

D'Este, Carlo. *Patton: a Genius for War.* New York: HarperCollins, 1995. Print.

Jenkins, Roy. *Churchill: a Biography.* New York: Farrar, Straus and Giroux, 2001. Print.

Lucas, James Sidney. *Command: a Historical Dictionary of Military Leaders.* New York: Military, 1988. Print.

Montagu, Ewen. *The Man Who Never Was.* Philadelphia: Lippincott, 1954. Print.

Sulzberger, C. L., David G. McCullough, and Ralph K. Andrist. *The American Heritage Picture History of World War II.* [New York]: American Heritage Pub., 1966. Print.

Whiting, Charles. *Patton.* New York: Ballantine, 1970. Print.

11

A Prisoner's Prayer

Corporal Jacob DeShazer (1942)

"But I say to you, love your enemies, bless those who curse you, do good to those who hate you, and pray for those who spitefully use you and persecute you."
Matthew 5:44(NKJV)

"We are in a tough situation fellas," the pilot's voice blared over the aircraft's intercom. The news was not a surprise to those aboard the *Bat out of Hell*, one of sixteen specially modified B-25 Mitchell bombers on a highly secretive mission. While only the pilot and co-pilot knew just how serious their fuel situation really was, the other three airmen could sense that things were bad.

The *Bat*, as the crew affectionately called their war bird, had been airborne now for thirteen straight hours. The plane's navigator, Lieutenant George Barr, for the past several hours, had been desperately trying to get a positive fix on their location. He could tell approximately where they were, but the overcast sky and the almost continuous fog over the China Sea, made navigation a real challenge.

Knowing their exact location was critical to the men onboard the *Bat.* Japanese forces occupied portions of China and, considering the mission they had just completed, the very last thing they wanted was to land or bail out anywhere near the Japanese Army.

The *Bat* had been the last aircraft in a sixteen plane task force to take off from the carrier, *USS Hornet,* at around nine o'clock that morning. Under the command of Lieutenant Colonel James "Jimmy" Doolittle, their mission was to bomb key targets in Japan, then fly across the ocean to China, where they would land at airfields in friendly territory, refuel and continue on to their rendezvous point at the airport in Chungking.

Lieutenant Bill Farrow, the pilot and Commander of the *Bat,* was assigned targets in the town of Nagoya. He was given discretion to choose the target; bombing industrial and military installations was acceptable, but under no circumstance were any of the aircraft to bomb or fire at commercial, residential or civilian structures.

Lieutenant Farrow arrived over Nagoya, and was greeted by a barrage of anti-aircraft fire. To get safely below the flack from the bursting anti-aircraft shells, Farrow put the *Bat* into a steep dive, and leveled off at an altitude just above the treetops. The *Bat* flew so close to the trees that some of the men were concerned they would collide with birds spooked by the sound of their engines. Within a few moments, Farrow spotted a prime target; an oil storage facility almost dead-ahead of them. He would have to gain altitude for the bomb run, so he climbed to about fifteen hundred feet and lined up with the target. Corporal Jacob DeShazer, the *Bat's* bombardier, placed his finger on the bomb release trigger, as he looked through the specially designed bombsite. When the cross-hairs were centered on the tank, DeShazer gently squeezed the trigger, releasing their deadly payload directly on one of the storage tanks. Within seconds, the tank erupted in a tremendous explosion, and several other tanks followed as their contents also erupted into enormous balls of flame. The *Bat* shuddered as the first shock waves from the explosion slammed into the fuselage.

Accelerating to escape the shock waves of additional explosions, Lieutenant Farrow and co-pilot Lieutenant Bob Hite, fought to maintain control of the aircraft. Just as they were about to descend back to treetop level, both pilots spotted another target. Without speaking, the airmen turned the bomber slightly to the left towards an aircraft factory, leveled off and, right on cue, Jacob DeShazzer released the remaining ordinance, scoring a direct hit on the factory's main building. With their bomb bay empty, it was time to get out of Japan and into friendlier territory; however, this would prove to be the most dangerous and challenging part of what would be a very long day.

The *Bat* trembled as another shock wave slammed into the plane, but this time it was from anti-aircraft shells exploding only a few yards away. Hite and Farrow dodged the exploding anti-aircraft shells, as they dove the twin engine bomber back down to tree top level, and made a direct course toward their predetermined escape route. As they neared the Japanese coast, they spotted two other planes that had expelled their bombs over other parts of the city and were already making their way across the ocean. Farrow attempted to follow, but as the weather quickly deteriorated, they lost sight of both planes in the haze.

The *Bat* was now in a solid overcast, with visibility down to zero. Farrow pushed the yoke forward, putting the plane into a steep dive toward the ocean below. At about five hundred feet above the rolling waves, the *Bat* broke out of the clouds and Farrow quickly leveled off. As they sped along just above the waves, Lieutenant Barr notified the flight crew that they were burning fuel much faster than they had anticipated. This was very unwelcome news, as they needed every ounce of fuel to make it into free China.

For hours, they flew just above the crest of the waves, searching for the coastline of China. Around seven-twenty in the evening, Lieutenant Barr's voice broke over the intercom, as he announced he could see a lighthouse ahead. Knowing the peaks of the mountains that lined the Chinese coast were hidden in the clouds, Lieutenant Farrow immediately pulled the *Bat* into a climb. The g-force of the steep climb pushed the crew members into their seats, as they struggled to hastily gain altitude. Finally, at what he felt was a safe altitude to clear any of the mountain peaks, Farrow leveled out at eleven thousand feet. Now over the mainland of China, Lieutenant Barr announced they should head directly to the city of Chuchow, and gave Farrow a new course heading. The pilot turned the *Bat* towards Chuchow, where a friendly airfield with desperately needed fuel awaited their arrival.

For the next three hours, DeShazer carefully watched Barr as he intently studied his charts, made numerous calculations and triple checked his coordinates. Intercom and radio chatter were kept to a minimum, so not to distract Barr's intense concentration. Their lives were in the hands of their navigator, and he desperately worked to get the pilots an exact location of where they were, where they should be heading, and whether they had enough fuel to get there. Lieutenant Farrow's voice sounded through the headset, interrupting Barr's concentration, as he announced they had less than one hour of fuel remaining.

It now was obvious they were not going to make it to Chuchow, so Farrow picked up the microphone and explained their situation to the crew.

"We are in a tough situation fellas. We obviously can't find Chuchow in this stuff and I'm not going to try to set down underneath it because I'm sure these clouds are full of rocks. We know free China is to the South and we know Chunking lies to the west, but too far away for the gas we've got."

Farrow released the microphone and the radio went silent. With no hope of making it to a friendly airport, he set a course toward the southwest, hoping to break out of the clouds and find a place to set down. A road, a rice paddy, or even a flat stretch of land would suffice; he just wanted to get his crew to safety and, if possible, save the aircraft. Completing a mission with the aircraft intact is a responsibility every pilot takes very seriously, but Farrow knew that saving the crew was the top priority, and the possibility of having to abandon their ship in flight was growing greater by the minute.

The low fuel indicator illuminated on the instrument panel, warned that the *Bat's* two engines would soon begin to cough, sputter and then go quiet. Farrow noticed a break in the clouds, and Barr announced that he could see the lights of a town below. Farrow quickly dove the *Bat* towards the clear skies below, as Barr grabbed his maps and compared the light patterns on the ground to his aviation chart. To their dismay, Barr positively identified the town below them as Nanchang.

The crew of the *Bat*, as well as other planes in the Raid, had been warned that Nanchang, and its surrounding area, was occupied by the Japanese; nevertheless, with the aircraft nearly out of fuel and no suitable place for a safe landing, Farrow was left with no other choice than to order the crew to begin preparations to bail out. As the crew donned their parachutes and retrieved their survival gear, one of the engines sputtered, which caused them all to move a little quicker.

Jacob DeShazer crawled from his bombardier's station in the nose of the plane, to a hatch where, upon Farrow's order, he would leap from the doomed aircraft. Jacob grabbed onto the side of the plane, and prepared to thrust himself out into the darkness. It was eleven forty in the evening when Lieutenant Farrow finally gave the order to bail out. At about three thousand feet above hostile territory, bombardier Jacob DeShazer hurled himself through the hatch and began a freefall into the incredibly dark and murky night.

At that moment, over five thousand miles away in Madres, Oregon Jacob's mother, Mrs. Hulda Andrus, was suddenly awakened from her sleep, feeling as if she was falling through the air. Along with this strange sensation, Mrs. Andrus also felt an urgent need to pray.

She had no idea that Jacob was in harm's way, as the last time she had spoken to him, he was stationed somewhere in the state of Florida. Without any idea that her son was, at that moment, plummeting through the dark night sky on the other side of the world, Mrs. Andrus immediately began praying for God to relieve her of this burden. She continued praying until the burden lifted, and she was able to return to a peaceful sleep.

OVER NANCHANG

It was so dark and foggy, Jacob could barely see his hands, much less anything around him. When he was sure he was clear of the aircraft, he began searching for the parachute's rip cord. He found it and pulled hard, releasing the parachute from its pack. The chute snapped open, and Jacob felt a sudden, but welcome, jerk as the silk canopy filled with air, rapidly slowing his descent. When Jacob looked up to ensure the chute had properly deployed, he caught a final glimpse of the now empty *Bat*, as it raced away overhead. He could see the plane's interior lights through the hatch from which he had just escaped. Soon the lights disappeared, and the roar of the motors subsided. Now there was only quiet.

The only sound Jacob could hear was the air rippling through the parachute as he descended through the night air. It was an eerie quiet, which gave Jacob a strange sense of loneliness. As Jacob literally hung by a few strings underneath a canopy of silk, he began to wonder about what awaited him below. Would he be captured? Would he be tortured or even executed? Surely news about the bombing of the Japanese homeland would have made it to the Japanese Army stationed around Nanchang. They would likely already have patrols out looking for the American airmen, since they would have easily been able to figure out the American bombers were heading towards China.

Jacob did not know what awaited him, but as he slowly descended through the night, he had time to think about his life and the events that had brought him to this moment.

STRIKING BACK

A little more than four months earlier, Jacob DeShazar was just getting comfortable with his new life. He was finally getting accustomed to the daily routine of an enlisted man in the Army Air Corps. It was not a bad life, especially during peacetime. Jacob had joined the Army eighteen months earlier, with hopes of fulfilling a lifelong dream of becoming a pilot. After completing his basic training, Jacob was given the unfortunate news that, according to Army regulations, at age twenty seven, he was too old to begin pilot training. Still wanting to fly, Jacob learned that the Army was looking for volunteers to attend bombardier training. Although he would not be a pilot, this would at least give him the opportunity to fly, so he volunteered and was soon on his way to bombardier school.

After training, Jacob was assigned to Camp Pendleton, Oregon where he went back to enjoying his peaceful life in the Army. On the Sunday afternoon of December 7, 1941, as Jacob was handling light duties in the base chow hall, events were unfolding in the middle of the Pacific Ocean, which were about to interrupt his comfortable routine and change his life forever.

Jacob was still working in the chow hall when the word of the attack at Pearl Harbor reached Camp Pendleton. The news enraged Jacob, and he shouted that the "Japs" would pay for their deeds. However, he did not realize that, within just a few short months, he would be part of the first strike of retaliation against Japan.

Following the attack at Pearl Harbor, life at Pendleton was less mundane; the United States was now at war. In the Pacific, Japan continued sweeping across the ocean, taking French-Indo China, Thailand, Malaya, Burma and Singapore. They took the Philippines, driving General Douglas MacArthur off the Island, and continued on to take Java, Borneo, New Britain, New Ireland and the Solomon Islands. It seemed as if nothing could stop the Japanese from controlling the entire Pacific.

While on duty one day, Jacob was notified that he was to report to the Captain. When Jacob reported, he found that about twenty others had also been summoned to the meeting. The Captain announced that he was looking for volunteers for a very dangerous and highly secretive mission. The mission is so dangerous, the captain informed them, that some will likely not make it back. Every man in the room, still enraged by the attack on Pearl Harbor, eagerly volunteered for the mission, including Jacob.

The volunteers were relocated to Eglin Field in northern Florida, where they were assigned to five-man crews. Jacob was teamed up with Pilot Lieutenant William "Bill" Farrow, Co-pilot Lieutenant Robert "Bob" Hite, Navigator Lieutenant George Barr, and Sergeant Harold Spaatz, who served as mechanic and gunner. Jacob would be the aircraft's bombardier, and it would ultimately be his responsibility to deliver to the Japanese, the retaliation for the damage they had inflicted at Pearl Harbor.

Not long after arriving at Eglin, the crews were introduced to their Commander, the famous and daring aviator, Lieutenant Colonel James "Jimmy" Doolittle. At their first meeting, Doolittle re-emphasized the danger of their mission, and the importance of secrecy. None of the volunteers knew anything about the mission, nor would they be informed until they were well on their way; but they were constantly reminded of the dangers. Each time Doolittle gathered them together, he gave them an opportunity to back out honorably. Even aboard the *USS Hornet*, just hours before the launch of their mission, Doolittle would again remind them of the dangers and offer for anyone to back out, without any retribution or dishonor.

For weeks the crews trained. Navy pilots were assigned to help train the Army pilots on the techniques of short runway take-offs, since Navy aviators were the experts at short launches. However, Naval aircraft were designed for such missions, unlike the B-25 Mitchells, flown by Doolittle's volunteers. These bombers were heavy land-based aircraft, and special modifications had to be made to lighten them so they could get airborne within the distance of an aircraft carrier's runway. Modifications were also made to extend the aircraft's fuel range.

One day Lt. Colonel Doolittle called the men together and told them to take care of their personal matters, as they would be shipping out very soon. Within a few days, the *Bat*, along with fifteen other B-25s, left Eglin Field and relocated to California. Once final adjustments were made to the aircraft in California, they were loaded aboard the *USS Hornet*, and Doolittle and his air crews set sail for a destination only known to a select few in the entire nation.

After a few days at sea, the *Hornet* rendezvoused with the *USS Enterprise*, which had sailed from Pearl Harbor to provide air cover in case the task force was detected by the Japanese. Then, Doolittle informed the crews of their historic mission. They were going to sail within four hundred miles of the Japanese mainland, and launch all sixteen aircraft. Their mission was to strike at the heart of the Japanese empire, bombing Tokyo and other Japanese cities. The Japanese believed they were invulnerable to attack because American Naval aircraft did not have the fuel range to attack and safely return to their carriers. The Japanese had also established a security net of naval vessels about two hundred miles around the island, to detect and prevent American aircraft carriers from getting within striking distance.

This was the reason Jacob and the others had been training to launch long range Army Air Corps bombers off the short runway of an aircraft carrier. With the long range B-25s, they would be able to launch much further out than their Navy counterparts, avoiding the Japanese safety net. Although the heavy bombers were now able to take off from a carrier, they could not land on the carrier's runways, so extra fuel tanks were installed aboard the B-25s to give them enough fuel to make it into free China, where they could land and refuel.

On April 18, 1942, just four months after the Japanese attack at Pearl Harbor, Jacob DeShazer climbed aboard his Mitchell bomber, headed for Japan. However, not much seemed to be going right for this mission. Due to the carrier being detected by a Japanese naval vessel, the mission had to be launched several hours earlier than planned, which meant they had an additional two hundred miles to fly just to reach Japan. The additional distance, steady headwinds, and bad weather all contributed to the *Bat* prematurely running out of fuel, and Jacob now parachuting into enemy territory in the middle of the night.

CAPTURED

Surrounded by foggy darkness, Jacob had no idea how far below him was the ground, nor did he know when or where he would land. After what seemed like an eternity of falling, Jacob anxiously waited for his feet to touch something solid. He hoped he would not land in one of the rice paddies that covered much of the Chinese countryside. He had been warned that the Chinese fertilized their fields with human excrement, and even the smallest scratch would be infected by the bacteria in the water.

Jacob suddenly hit the ground hard, on top of a mound of dirt. He immediately threw his arms around the dirt pile and gave it a welcome hug. As his eyes adjusted to the darkness, he realized he was surrounded by several similar dirt mounds; Jacob had landed in a Chinese cemetery. As he moved to stand up, Jacob felt a sharp pain in his chest, and thought that he must have broken a few ribs when he hit the grave. He took out his knife, cut himself loose from his parachute, and began to search for shelter. Soon he found a small brick building, a Chinese shrine, where he spent the night.

The next morning, Jacob set out on foot looking for a village or someone who could help him. He happened upon a group of soldiers who were playing with some local children. Not sure if he was in a Japanese occupied area, Jacob cautiously approached the soldiers and asked, "China or Japan?" "China," a soldier replied, as another soldier turned and quickly left the group. This made Jacob uneasy, and he decided it would be best to be on his way but, as he walked away, another soldier called for him to come back. Nervously, Jacob returned and was invited to enter a small shed. As Jacob walked into the dark room, he was surrounded by eight to ten soldiers with guns and advised, by one of the soldiers who spoke English, that he was now a prisoner of Japan.

Jacob, the other four men from the *Bat*, and three men from the *Green Hornet*, the fifth plane in the task force, had all been captured. They were rounded up by Chinese guerrillas, handed over to the Japanese Army, and transported to a an enemy prison camp, where they were soon subjected to their first rounds of interrogation and torture.

After several weeks of various forms of brutal torture, the weakened and starving American aviators were taken before a military court and, through the proceedings of a mock trial, they were declared guilty of murder. The Japanese military had falsely reported that the *Doolittle Raiders* had purposefully targeted schools and hospitals during their attack on Japan. They manufactured reports that the Raiders had specifically machine-gunned school children while they were playing in their school yards, as well as hospitals and orphanages. Of course, Jacob and his comrades knew this was all fabricated, but when they protested, they were only subjected to more beatings.

As the judge ended the trial, the men were told their sentences through an interpreter. All eight were found guilty and were to be executed for crimes against the Japanese people. Following the trial, they were moved to another prison where seven of them were held in solitary confinement. Lieutenant Hallmark, the pilot of the *Green Hornet*, had become extremely ill with dysentery and was taken to another prison where he was placed in a cell with twenty other prisoners of various nationalities. All of the captured Raiders patiently endured the deplorable conditions, poor food, and stench of their own bodies and the prison cells, as they awaited their executions.

On October 10, 1942, after nearly five months of imprisonment, a message was sent by the Chief of the Imperial General

Staff to the Commanding General of the China Expeditionary Force, notifying him that five of the American's sentences were being commuted to life imprisonment. However, Jacobs's pilot, Lieutenant Farrow, and the gunner, Sergeant Spaatz were to be executed along with the pilot of the *Green Hornet*, Lieutenant Hallmark. Their reason was that the pilots were directly responsible for flying the planes to the targets, and Sergeant Spaatz, the gunner, would have purposely gunned Japanese civilians. Even though Jacob, a bombardier, was also responsible for inflicting damage on Japan; for some reason, he was going to live.

It had been six months since Jacob and his buddies took off from the *USS Hornet*, and, throughout this time, Jacob had endured tremendous pain at the hands of his Japanese captors. The guards were ruthless, at times kicking and punching the defenseless and weakened American flyers. Jacob began developing a hatred for the Japanese, especially the Japanese military. He and the other three Raiders with him had been transferred to several prisons in China and Japan, and currently they were being held in solitary confinement in a prison near Tokyo. Their cells measured only nine by five feet, and there was no window, only a small opening near the ceiling. Guards were positioned at the door, where they would often taunt the prisoners and poke at them with long poles stuck through the opening in the door. When winter came, the cells were extremely cold and, with only one single blanket between their bodies and the cold floor, they shivered each night as they tried to sleep.

The horrible conditions and poor nutrition caused each man to develop various illnesses, which caused their bodies to further deteriorate; but the poor food, cold, and mistreatment was not the worst part of their imprisonment. The solitary confinement, being totally alone for twenty-three and a half hours a day, was the most torturous for the men. Although their cells were close together, if they attempted to communicate with each other, the guards would quickly enter their cells and beat them. For half an hour each day, Jacob and his comrades were let out into the exercise yard. They were not allowed to speak to each other during this time, but just being together gave them strength.

For some unknown reason, all four men were suddenly moved into a single cell. Although they were not permitted to speak, they communicated a bit through whispers, but mostly they just enjoyed being in one another's company. To break the monotony of their confinement, they developed games such as the "Flea-Lice-Catch," which they played every Sunday morning with great excitement. They would stack all their blankets into pile in the middle of the cell and, at the signal 'go' they would take a blanket and look for the tiny insects. They would receive one point for each louse, since they were easy to see and moved relatively slowly. A flea earned five points, since they were much harder to catch. At the end of the game, the prisoner with the most points received a portion of the other men's rations.

The men stayed together in the same cell until a day before the one year anniversary of their raid on Tokyo. On April 17, 1943 the men were led into the exercise yard, handcuffed and blindfolded. Realizing the significance of the following day, the men were afraid that the Japanese were going to acknowledge the anniversary of the raid with a public execution. However, instead of being led before a firing squad, they were taken to an airfield where they were loaded onto a plane and flown back to

Nanking, where they would endure two more years of hellish imprisonment.

CONVERSION

Upon arriving in Nanking, the four Raiders were once again placed in solitary confinement. While their new guards were not quite as vicious as the guards in the Tokyo prisons, Jacob and the others were still subjected to significant abuse, deprivation and beatings.

After twelve months as prisoners of war, the four were learning to tolerate the abuse and malnutrition; however, the worst punishment they experienced was the lack of mental activity. In the Nanking prison, they were isolated for all but fifteen minutes every day. Once a day they were taken to the exercise yard, one at a time, for a fifteen minute exercise period.

Although their physical conditions were slightly better, with almost total isolation from any other human being, their mental conditions began to rapidly deteriorate. Each of the men began experiencing intense hallucinations, mostly visions of things they most desperately needed, such as food and companionship. Often they would see images of large plates of food sitting on the floor of the cell, or imagine friends and loved ones coming by for visits. In some instances, their hallucinations would last for hours, only then to be disrupted by guards, who would enter the cells and shake or hit them to bring them back to reality.

In September, 1943 Bob Meder became very ill. The others realized that Bob was in serious condition when they would see him during their weekly baths, the only time they were together. On December 1, while making his morning rounds, a guard found Lieutenant Meder lying dead on the floor of his cell. With the death of Meder, obviously due to mistreatment, the Japanese began to slightly improve the conditions for the others. They began receiving a little bread with their meager rations, and the meals increased from two to three per day.

The most significant improvement came when they were given a few books to read. The prison commander, responding to the prisoner's requests for reading material, sent a soldier to a local bookstore to purchase books written in English. The soldier returned with five books which, likely quite unintentionally, were all Christian-themed. These books were given to the three remaining Raiders, and all were given an opportunity to read all five books. While each of the books had a significant positive impact upon the morale of these men, there was one book that made the greatest impression. It not only affected these men's current spiritual health, but it would set in place a series of events that would one day affect thousands of Japanese citizens, as well. That book was the *Holy Bible*.

Being the only enlisted man, Jacob was the last to receive the copy of the Bible. Finally in May, 1944 Jacob got his turn; and he eagerly began reading. He studied the Bible, reading it through several times, absorbing its message of hope and strength. As long as there was light enough to see, Jacob was reading the scriptures.

This was not the first time Jacob had read the Bible. Being raised in a Christian home and his father being a lay minister in the Methodist church, Jacob had learned about Christ as a child, but had fallen away from his faith when he left home as a teenager. Now reading the Bible again, in the isolation of his captivity, the scriptures were ministering to Jacob in a way he had never experienced before. Jacob was re-learning the faith he had been taught as a child.

About three weeks after receiving the Bible, Jacob read Romans 10:9 "If you confess with your mouth, Jesus is Lord; and believe in your heart that God raised him from the dead, you will be saved." These words burned deep in Jacobs's heart. During his three weeks of studying in solitary confinement, God had been ministering to Jacob through His word, and now Jacob was ready to give his heart and his life to Jesus Christ. Alone in his cell, without a minister delivering a sermon, without a choir, without an organ and without a formal alter-call, Jacob knelt by the small wooden stool in his cell and gave his life to Jesus. From this point forward, Jacob DeShazer's life was forever changed. Though he was renewed on the inside, the situation of his imprisonment and mistreatment had not changed, and Jacob's faith would soon be challenged.

One day, as Jacob was being escorted back to his cell after his short exercise period, a guard began hitting Jacob on the back and yelling at him to hurry up. When they reached the door to Jacob's cell, the guard shoved Jacob through the door, knocking him to the ground. Jacob's foot was still in the doorway when the guard slammed the cell door, catching Jacob's foot between the door and the jamb. Jacob felt a sharp pain as the door crushed his foot. Instead of opening the door so Jacob could free his foot, the guard pushed on the door and began kicking his foot. The pain was almost unbearable, and Jacob was once again feeling anger and hatred welling up inside of him, as the guard continued to kick his foot. Finally, Jacobs's foot broke free and, as he lay in his cell in tremendous pain, he remembered

Jesus' words, that we are to 'love our enemies and pray for those who abuse us.'

The tortures and abuse continued throughout the year and into the extremely cold winter. In June 1945, Jacob and the other two Raiders were suddenly taken from their cells, hand-cuffed and hoods placed over their heads. They were marched out of the prison, put on a truck and taken to the train station, where they boarded a passenger train.

They traveled under the watchful eyes of prison guards for three days until they finally arrived in Peking, China, where they were put in another prison. This time, the men were kept in their cells twenty-four hours a day. The only time they left the confinement of their small cells, was once a week for a bath.

On August 10, 1945 after an extended illness, Jacob awoke with a strong burden to pray. As he knelt on the cold hard floor of his cell, he felt the Holy Spirit compel him to pray for the peace of Japan.

Jacob had spent a lot of time praying since giving his life to Christ in Nanking, but he had never prayed for the peace of his captors. For forty months, the Japanese had mistreated, abused and tortured him and his comrades. They had even killed Lieutenant Meder. Until now, he had felt it was useless to pray for an end to the war, when he and his friends had so many pressing needs, such as healing for their sicknesses, strength to endure their punishment, and protection from the guards. But now God was directing him to pray for peace.

Without knowing exactly why, Jacob began praying that the leaders of Japan would desire peace. After seven hours of praying, Jacob suddenly felt the Holy Spirit say, "You don't need to pray any more, the victory is won."

Without a radio or news, other than the propaganda of the Japanese guards, which daily informed the Raiders that America was losing the war, Jacob had no idea what was transpiring outside the walls of his cell. However, just a few days earlier, the United States Army Air Corps had dropped the atomic bomb on Japan and, during the time Jacob was praying, Japanese military leaders were considering whether they should surrender to the Americans, or continue fighting.

Jacob did not know the purpose of his prayers, nor if they had an effect, but he had a new attitude. Without any identifiable reason, Jacob experienced a feeling of victory, as if the war was over and he and the others would soon be set free from their bondage. It would be several weeks before Jacob and the other two Raiders would learn about the bombs, and the subsequent surrender of Japan, but Jacob, although still physically weak, felt totally alive in his spirit.

One day as he was lying on his mat praying, the Holy Spirit once again spoke to Jacob saying, "You are called to go and teach the Japanese people, and go wherever I send you." For Jacob, showing love and mercy towards those who had caged him and treated him worse than an animal, would be very difficult. He knew this would really test his new found Christian faith, but he had committed to follow God wherever he would lead; and, if he made it out of prison, Jacob was willing to return to Japan.

Ten days after praying for the peace of Japan, Jacob's cell door opened, and a guard announced that the war was over. As the guard left, he did not close the door behind him, and Jacob freely walked out of his cell to meet the other Raiders.

The Raiders were taken by truck to an English hotel in Peking, where they were allowed to bathe, and were given haircuts and clothing. Shortly thereafter, several American commandos arrived at the hotel and, after four years of captivity, the three Doolittle Raiders were headed home.

MEETING WITH THE ENEMY

After returning to the United States, Jacob continued to feel the calling of God to be a missionary. It was extraordinary how God was changing his heart from the cold hatred he felt as a prisoner of war, to love, and a desire to share the love of Jesus Christ with the Japanese. Jacob heeded God's call, and six years and eight months after Jacob had boarded the *USS Hornet* as a bombardier, he once again found himself boarding a ship destined for Japan. On his first trip across the Pacific Ocean, Jacob was an angry young man who was seeking revenge for the attack on America, but this time, he was not armed with bombs, but with the gospel of Christ. The hatred he had felt in his heart as a prisoner of Japan, had been replaced with a passion for a lost people who needed God's hope and love.

While Jacob was attending seminary at Seattle Pacific College in Washington State, the Bible Meditation League produced a four page pamphlet about his life. The pamphlet was entitled "I was a prisoner of Japan," and was printed in over twenty languages and distributed to churches all around the world. Several thousand of these were distributed throughout Japan. Before Jacob even arrived, the Japanese people were already familiar with Jacob DeShazer and his experiences.

Once settled in Osaka, Jacob began speaking at meetings around the city. At one particular event, Jacob had an encounter that suddenly brought back the memories and feelings of his captivity. Jacob was speaking at the town theater in Osaka, to an audience mostly comprised of families who had lost a loved one in the war. There were also a large number of Japanese war veterans in attendance. As Jacob concluded his remarks, he noticed a familiar face in the back of the room. Jacob left the stage and walked towards the back. Drawing closer, his eyes met with the familiar face, and Jacob's mind was instantly taken back to the prison cell in Nanking. He recognized the face as that of Captain Kudo, the prison guard who had slammed the door on Jacob's foot, and kicked him into the cell.

Jacob walked directly towards the man that had so abused him in prison. As he approached Captain Kudo, Jacob stuck out his hand, and the two former enemies shook hands as if they were friends. Jacob's face broke out in a big smile, showing Kudo that all was forgiven. Kudo responded to this kind gesture, telling Jacob that he had been reading the Bible and was learning about Christianity.

A year and a half after meeting Captain Kudo, Jacob was told that another former military officer had requested to meet with him. This officer had been a pilot during the war and, although they had never met, the impact of Jacob's testimony had led this man to accept Christ. Jacob learned that the former officer had been given one of his pamphlets while waiting on a train in Tokyo. He had started to discard it but, realizing that Jacob was one of the Doolittle Raiders, he felt compelled to read it. As Jacob was also an airman, he was inspired to read about how Jacob, motivated by the attack on Pearl Harbor, had volunteered for a dangerous mission to bomb Japan. He read about Jacob's capture, torture and mistreatment, and about how Jacob had forgiven the Japanese and was now living and ministering in Japan.

Jacob was told that this man was so inspired by his story that he wanted to know more about him and this God he spoke of, so he bought a book about Jacob's life. He then purchased a Bible and began to study it, just as Jacob had while in prison. Through Jacob's testimony, this man had become a Christian and now wanted to meet and pray with Corporal Jacob DeShazer, one of Doolittle's Raiders.

Later that afternoon, the former Japanese pilot arrived at Jacobs home, escorted by another American missionary and a Japanese interpreter. As he opened the door, the interpreter asked if he was Jacob DeShazer. "I am," he replied. "Mr. DeShazer," the interpreter said," this is Mistuo Fuchida, the pilot who led the attack on Pearl Harbor, and he would like to thank you for your testimony." After talking for some time about their experiences, the commander of the attack on Pearl Harbor and the Doolittle Raider knelt down together and prayed.

Fuchida would eventually become a minister, preaching the gospel of Christ throughout the nation of Japan. Since Fuchida was a national hero, his testimony had a great influence on the people of Japan. Through his preaching, thousands of Japanese people were led to accept Christ as their Savior. Fuchida often said that it was because Jacob was a fellow airman, and a Doolittle Raider, that he read the pamphlet he was given at the train station. It was the similarity of the two men's lives that influenced Fuchida to further explore the faith that caused Jacob to forgive and love his enemies.

Throughout their remaining years, each of these war heroes shared a great admiration for the other, and after many years of ministering the gospel of Jesus Christ, both men commented that their first meeting was a highlight of their lives.

A strange but providential chain of events had put Jacob DeShazer in a position to influence a national hero of Japan to accept Christ. It was that small Bible, given to him by Japanese prison guards and read in a cold lonely prison cell, that eventually led thousands of Japanese citizens to Christianity.

References

Bradley, James, *Flyboys, A True Story of Courage*. New York, New York: Little Brown and Company, 2003

Benge, Janet and Geoff, *Jacob DeShazer, Forgive Your Enemies*. Seattle, Washington: YWAM Publishing. 1958.

Cohen, Stan. *East Wind Rain, A Pictorial History of the Pearl Harbor Attack*. Missoula, Montana: Pictorial Histories Publishing Company.

Glines, Carroll, V. *Four Came Home, The gripping story of the survivors of Jimmy Doolittles two lost crews*. Missoula, Montana: Pictorial Histories Publishing Company, 1966.

Glines, Carroll, V. *The Doolittle Raid, America's daring first strike against Japan*. Atglen, Pennsilvania: Shiffer Publishing Ltd, 1991.

Goldstein, Donald M. and Dixon, Carol Aido Deshazer, *Return of the Raider, A Doolittle Raider's story of War and Forgiveness*. Lake Mary, Florida; Creation House,, 2010.

Prange, Gordon, W. *God's Samurai, Lead Pilot at Park Harbor*, Washington, DC: Brassey's, Inc. 1990.

Wels, Susan, *December 7, 1941 Pearl Harbor, America's Darkest Day*. San Diego, California: Laurel Glen Publishing, 2001,

12

A Change of Heart

General Lew Wallace (1878)

"Trust in the Lord with all thine heart: And lean not unto thine own understanding. In all thy ways acknowledge him, And he shall direct thy paths."
Proverbs 3:5-6

The setting sun was casting long rays of red and orange light, illuminating the sky with fire like luminescence. Governor Lew Wallace always enjoyed the New Mexico sunsets, and would often set aside his writing to watch the bright orange sun dip below the barren landscape. Other than the time he spent pursuing his passion of writing, these picturesque sunsets were the only peaceful escape he found from the stresses of governing the often hostile New Mexico Territory.

As the last of the sun's rays disappeared below the horizon, Governor Wallace returned to his desk, lit a lamp and resumed his work. Although he governed one of the most violent territories of the country, Wallace found time to pursue his passion of writing. The novel he had begun back in his hometown, Crawfordsville, Indiana, over six years ago, was nearing completion and Wallace worked late into most evenings editing the manuscript. He was spending every available moment, not taken by his official duties, in preparing his work for publication. In a letter to his wife in November, 1879 Wallace wrote, "I am busy putting in every spare minute copying my book for publication. It is curious this jumping from the serious things of life to the purely romantic. It is like nothing so much as living two lives in one."

While the governor carefully transcribed his thoughts and ideas into a meaningful manuscript, a friend quietly stepped into the room and closed the window shutters, so the Governor could not be seen from the streets outside. In the short time he had served as Governor, Wallace had become a target of many of the outlaw gangs that roamed the New Mexico wilderness.

General Lew Wallace had been appointed by President Rutherford B. Hayes in September of 1878, to serve as Territorial Governor of the New Mexico Territory. Unlike many other government appointments, this one was not a political favor. The previous governor, Samuel Axtell, had been financially involved in illegal activities with two businessmen in Lincoln County. A federal agent with the Department of the Interior, who investigated the crimes, described Axtell's inept administration as having more "corruption, fraud, mismanagement, plots and murder" than any other Governor in our nation's history. Axtell was removed from office, and President Hayes set out to find a trusted and loyal leader who would clean up the corruption and violence created by the Axtell administration. President Hayes selected General Lew Wallace, a veteran of the Union Army, who held a high moral character and had proven effective as a military and political leader.

The President directed Wallace to clean up the corrupt New Mexico government, and restore law and order to this virtually lawless part of the country. Wallace held a unique set of qualifications that would prove to be useful in this position. As the youngest General in the Union Army during the Civil War, Wallace had shown himself to be a strong military leader. He commanded the Third Division of the Army of Tennessee during the Battle of Shiloh, and was later hailed as the "Savior of Cincinnati" for his daring defense of that city. President Abraham Lincoln had Wallace appointed as commander of the Eighth Army Corps where, with a force of only 5,800 soldiers, he made a heroic stand against General Jubal Early and his 18,000 Confederates at the Monocacy River in Maryland. Even though Wallace eventually lost the Battle of Monacacy Junction, delaying the Confederate march towards Washington D.C. had given General Ulysses S. Grant time to move reinforcements into the city. Wallace's brave stand at Monocacy Junction saved the nation's capitol from falling into the hands of the Confederates, and Wallace's fame quickly spread throughout the nation.

Following the war, General Lew Wallace continued to gain national prominence, as he was selected to serve on the commission that investigated and tried the conspirators involved in the assassination of President Lincoln. He also served on the court martial board that tried Captain Henry Wirtz, the Confederate commandant in charge of the notorious prison camp at Andersonville, Georgia. With his popularity in military and political circles escalating, Wallace also gained recognition in the literary world as a prominent writer. His first published book entitled *The Fair God,* was a novel about the conquest of the Aztec Empire by the Spanish. Although sales of the book were only moderate, it received positive reviews from the literary elite, and established General Lew Wallace as a respected American author.

LINCOLN COUNTY WARS

Serving as governor of an area that would eventually be synonymous with America's wild west, required more of Wallace's military experience than his skill as a politician. Lincoln County, located in the south central portion of the territory, was the hotbed of violence in America's western expansion.

During the late 1870s, competition between two Lincoln County businesses turned violent, and virtually everyone in the county allied with one side or the other. Lawrence Murphy and James Dolan had successfully built a business monopoly in Lincoln County, and used any means necessary to protect it, including murder. The corrupt administration of Governor Axtell had awarded the LG Murphy Company a contract to supply beef to the federal government; however, most of the beef they provided was illegally obtained through cattle rustling.

In 1876, an Englishman named John Tunstall, with the support of a local cattle rancher, John Chisum, and attorney Alexander McSween, opened a general store in Lincoln. Since Murphy owned or controlled all other businesses in the county, a feud erupted which resulted in the murder of John Tunstall. Sheriff William Brady, who was also controlled by the Murphy mob, sent a posse of outlaws to shut down Tunstall's business operations and confiscate his property. However, when the posse happened upon Tunstall herding horses back to Lincoln, they shot and killed him. From there, the violence escalated into an all out shooting war, and Lincoln's main street became known as the most dangerous street in America.

Fortunately, Governor Wallace had apprehended one of the territory's most notorious outlaws, William H. Boney, who was also one of the key participants in the Lincoln County Wars. Better known by his nickname, *Billy the Kid*, Boney had been arrested and placed in protective custody in the Lincoln County jail. Billy was a participant and eye witness to the murder of Sheriff William Brady, by a gang known as the *Regulators*. The *Regulators* were employees and associates, loyal to John Tunstall, who set out to seek revenge for their boss's murder. Through a series of letters, Governor Lew Wallace convinced Billy to testify in the trial and, in return, the governor promised amnesty for Billy's part in this crime. However, Wallace, unwilling to let a confessed killer go totally free, insisted that Billy would still remain accountable for his previous offenses.

When the Lincoln County trials finally commenced, Billy did just as he had promised, and testified before the grand jury against his fellow *Regulators*. But instead of being released from custody as Billy expected, the District Attorney kept him in prison. Billy wrote to Governor Wallace, accusing him of breaking their agreement, stating that he was promised a full pardon. Wallace replied that he had only extended amnesty for the crimes relating to the murder of Sheriff Brady, and Billy would be tried for his other offenses. Believing he had been double crossed by Wallace, Billy escaped from prison and returned to life as an outlaw. In response, Governor Wallace retracted all offers of amnesty and ordered Billy to be tracked down, captured, and returned to jail to face trial. In December of 1880, *Billy the Kid* was tracked down by Sheriff Pat Garret and, after a long standoff, Billy finally surrendered and was returned to the Lincoln County jail to await trial.

When the date of the trial finally arrived, Billy was escorted, under heavy guard, from his cell to the courtroom where he faced charges for the murder of three men. After brief deliberations, the jury acquitted him on the first two counts, but on the third count they delivered a "guilty" verdict, and subsequently *Billy the Kid* was sentenced to death by hanging. Shortly after the trial, General Wallace, at the desk where he had spent countless hours working on his latest novel, took his pen in hand and wrote the death warrant for one of America's most famous outlaws.

Shortly after his conviction, with the help of accomplices, Billy shot his way out of jail and escaped. Billy had a gang of admirers and followers who were more than willing to help him get revenge. Billy threatened that, once he killed Sheriff Pat Garret and the judge who sentenced him, he would also gun down Governor Wallace, who double crossed him. Because of this and other such threats, the Governor's friends and staff would ensure the window blinds were closed every evening and they would often stay up late to help protect Wallace as he wrote.

Governor Wallace was not fond of his life as a frontier governor, but he was sent to do a job, and he meant to do it well. "This way of living does not suit me," he wrote to his wife Susan, "some men find an unaccountable fascination in the danger and outlawry of the frontier far beyond my understanding." Although he did not care for the threats and violence that came with his job, Wallace found solace in his writing. In describing his zeal for writing, Wallace explained, "I know what I should love to do – to build a study; to write, and to think of nothing else. I want to bury myself in a den of books. I want to saturate myself with the elements of which they are made..."

By bringing law and order to the New Mexico Territory, Wallace had once again gained national recognition. Although his accomplishments as territorial governor, his heroic actions in the war, his participation in high profile post war commissions, or one of his several U.S. Patents, alone, would have ensured his place in America's history, it would be his literary skill and a single work of fiction that would bring him worldwide notoriety.

Wallace was nearing completion of his second book, a novel he had been writing for over six years. While his first book gained him acceptance among the literary elite, it would be this book that would catapult him to fame. The story was both entertaining and inspiring, with plots of friendship, betrayal, revenge, love, forgiveness, and plenty of action. It would eventually become the bestselling book of the nineteenth century, as well as being adapted into several stage plays. The popularity of this book would long outlive its author, entertaining and inspiring future audiences; however, the manuscript he was working on now was a much different story than the one he began writing many years earlier.

A TRAIN BOUND FOR GLORY

After the War Between the States, Wallace, like many former Army officers, turned his attentions from warfare to politics. He moved back to his hometown of Crawfordsville, Indiana and, upon learning that the 1876 Republican Convention was going to be held in nearby Indianapolis, he decided to attend. Wallace purchased a bunk on the evening train from Crawfordsville to Indianapolis, hoping to get some rest during the two hour trip. However, by way of providence, General Lew Wallace met an old friend on the train, and their conversation would inevitably change the course of his life and his writing.

After boarding the evening train, Wallace stumbled along a narrow hallway until he found his sleeper compartment. He stowed his luggage and made his way toward the dining car. As Wallace passed the luxurious state-room compartment, he heard someone call his name, followed by a knock on the window. The door to the compartment opened and there stood an old army acquaintance, Colonel Robert G. Ingersoll, who served under Wallace during the war, and Ingersoll invited Wallace to join him in his compartment for a visit.

Following the war, Colonel Ingersoll's notoriety had also risen, but under significantly different circumstances than those of General Wallace. Throughout the war, it was well known among the ranks that Ingersoll was a devout atheist. He would often engage in conversation with other officers about their religious beliefs, and attempt to draw them into debate. Following the war, he had continued promoting his atheism and, as Wallace soon realized, Ingersoll was still enthusiastic about his beliefs and eager to share his views on religion with anyone who would listen. He had spent the past several years on the lecture circuit, where huge crowds attended his lectures, and he was considered the nation's foremost authority on atheism. Ingersoll enjoyed debating the issue of the existence of God with most anyone willing to take on the task; though with Wallace, it was not necessary to debate, as he knew that Wallace also questioned God's existence.

From reading Wallace's first book, *The Fair God,* Ingersoll recognized Wallace had a talent for writing, and he had an idea he eagerly wanted to discuss with Wallace. Since he was desirous of companionship, Wallace joined his old friend and, as usual, they began to discuss the subject of religion. The conversation quickly turned to the existence, or better yet, the non-existence of God. As was typical, Colonel Ingersoll did most of the talking. For two hours Ingersoll spoke about what Wallace described as a "medley of argument, eloquence, wit, satire, audacity, irreverence, poetry, brilliant antitheses, and pungent excoriation of believers in God, Christ, and Heaven, the like of which I had never heard."

As the train arrived in Indianapolis, Ingersoll suggested that Wallace should write a story exposing Jesus as just an ordinary man and dispel the myth of his Divinity. As the two men parted ways, Wallace committed to Ingersoll that he would consider the venture.

Wallace walked to his brother's home, which was some distance from the train station and, as he walked alone in the dark, he pondered the conversation with Ingersoll, and his proposal. He thought about how little he really knew about the subject of God, heaven, the hereafter and Jesus. The importance of such an effort struck him and he considered taking on the project; however, Wallace did not just write stories without significant research. In his previous book, he immersed himself in the lives and history of his subjects before he attempted to write their story. His first book took twenty-five years to research and write, and this project would require no less of an effort.

A Revelation

As he continued walking, he thought about what Ingersoll had said, as well as the many sermons he had heard preached by some of the most noted ministers of his time. He was impressed by their oratory skills, their literary charm, and their knowledge, but none of them moved him the way this non-believer had stirred his emotions. He felt ashamed that he knew so little about the subject of God. Although he professed "neither a belief nor disbelief" in God or Christ, he realized that he had never given the subject much thought or research. A few years earlier Wallace had written a short story about the birth of Jesus. Although he admitted to being an agnostic and "was not in the least influenced by religious sentiment," he had a fascination with the story of Christ's birth. He thought about the manuscript filed away in a desk drawer at his home, and decided he should continue that story through to the crucifixion of Jesus.

Upon returning to his home in Crawfordsville, Wallace pulled the manuscript from his desk drawer and immediately set to work on continuing the story. Since "preachers had no impression" upon him regarding the existence of God, and he shuddered at the thought of delving into theology, he determined he would go to the Bible, specifically the four gospels, for his research. Since he was indifferent to the existence of God, Wallace had no intention of writing from a religious viewpoint. He wanted to expose his supposition that the religious and political situation of the world under Roman rule "demonstrated the necessity for a Savior." He decided to build characters that knew of this man called Jesus, without ever giving the reader direct accounts of the man. He would show that, because of Roman domination, the Jews, who so desired a Savior, were vulnerable to the claims that the man named Jesus was their Messiah.

While the final chapters were written in the Palace of Governors in Santa Fe, New Mexico, most of the research and writing took place on a rocking chair with a lap board under the shade of a gigantic beech tree in Crawfordsville. As he developed the story, he regularly read the four gospels of the New Testament to learn more of this man, Jesus. As he wrote, the characters of his book became like living persons to him. "They arise and sit, look, talk and behave like themselves," Wallace said. "In dealing with them I see them; when they speak I hear them. I know them by their features. They answer my call."

Wallace believed that, as a non-believer, he was at a disadvantage and his research "had to be so painstaking," because the subject of Jesus was known more thoroughly by scholars than any other subject in the world. Never having traveled to the Holy Land, he had to rely on books, maps and periodicals in bringing the Middle East alive in the minds of his readers. He traveled to Washington D.C. and Boston "for no purpose but to exhaust their libraries" for details of architecture and the structure of Roman sea craft. He interviewed travelers who had visited the Holy Land, to acquire details of birds, flowers, vegetation, and seasons. However, the Bible remained his most referenced authority on the life and times of Jesus and those who were called his Disciples.

Wallace knew that the Christian community would never tolerate a work of fiction with Jesus as the hero, but somehow He would have to be a focus of the story. Jesus would have to appear and speak to the characters, but Wallace decided that He would not speak or act directly. He would withhold the appearance of Jesus until the very end, but He would always be a part of the story. Jesus would be spoken of or he would be coming, but always as if he were "just over the hill yonder," and will be here tomorrow. Any words of Jesus would have to be "a literal quotation from one of his sainted biographers," which Wallace would obtain directly from the scripture.

Wallace became obsessed with writing this story, and desired to spend his every waking hour researching and writing; but, because he also held full time employment as a lawyer, he had to write as time allowed. Sometimes the thoughts of his characters were so strong, it was as if they were calling him to write the next lines of their story, and he would "play truant from court and clients" to pacify them. Countless hours were spent writing, on trains between cities or waiting in stations.

As he continued his research of historical documents and books, he gradually came to the knowledge that Jesus of Nazareth did indeed exist during this time in history. The thought began to weigh on Wallace's mind that, since Jesus did exist, might He also have been the Messiah that He claimed to be. Wallace found himself unwillingly departing from the agnostic criticism he had originally purposed, and was "writing more reverently and frequently with awe."

Tremendous unrest regarding the Divinity of Christ pursued General Lew Wallace, until one day he finally succumbed to the truth and, falling to his knees he "cried for the pardon of his unbelief." It is unknown exactly when Jesus reached through the chapters and verses of the scripture; but somewhere during the writing of Ben Hur, Wallace came to the realization that God was real, and that Jesus was the Son of God. Just like the main character of his story, *Judah Ben Hur*, this new revelation of

Christ took Wallace's life and his story in a new direction. His conversion came without a preacher's sermon to move him emotionally or a professor's lecture on theology to inspire his thought. Unaware at the time, Wallace had been daily walking with Jesus through the study of His story in the Bible.

Ingersoll taught that the horrors of war, the evils of a corrupt government and all the lawlessness General Wallace experienced, was evidence that we live in a world without God. But General Lew Wallace learned that, although we live in a world of sin, there is a God and he sent us a Savior, His son Jesus Christ.

Since its first publication in November of 1880, the story of *Ben Hur* has never been out of print, and holds the record as the second most published book in history. Only the Bible, the original story of Christ, has sold more copies. Lew Wallace's story of Christ became one of the most successful literary works in world history, and Wallace acknowledged that there were actually two successes from his writing, "First," said Wallace, "the book *Ben Hur,* and second, a conviction amounting to absolute belief in God and the Divinity of Christ."

It is ironic that one of the most published and read Christian stories in the history of the world was actually inspired by the encouragement of an atheist. Although Wallace intended to cast doubt on the divinity of Christ, the truth severed the darkness of doubt and, seeing the light, General Lew Wallace fell on his knees, and prayed.

REFERENCES

Kerr, Alva M., ed "Had to Write a Different Book." *The Herald of Gospel Liberty* 113.45 (1921): 1.Print.

Tan, Paul Lee. *Encyclopedia of 15,000 Illustrations: Signs of the times.* Dallas, TX: Bible Communications, 1998. Print

Wallace, Lew, and William Martin Johnson. *The First Christmas, from "Ben Hur,"* New York: Harper & Bros., 1902. Print.

Wallace, Lew. *Lew Wallace; an Autobiography.* New York: Harper & Brothers, 1906. Print.

13

A MARTYR FOR FREEDOM

Captain Nathan Hale (1776)

"Greater love hath no man than this, that a man lay down his life for his friends."
John 15:13

General William Howe, Commander in Chief of the British forces, notified his Provost Marshall, William Cunningham, to report immediately to the British Headquarters at the Beekman Estate. It was Saturday afternoon, September 21, 1776 when Cunningham arrived at the British headquarters, located in a rural part of New York's Manhattan Island. A captured American rebel was about face trial for spying, and General Howe knew Cunningham could be trusted to impose the most harsh and rightful punishment.

The accused was a handsome young man who stood over six feet tall and appeared to be in excellent physical condition. He was dressed in brown pants and coat, and wore a large brimmed felt hat, much like the ones popular with the Dutch who populated the coastal areas of Long Island. Other than a small scar on his face, obviously a burn from the flash powder of a musket, he could pass as one of the local residents. He claimed to be a Dutch school teacher seeking a position in New York. He was carrying a diploma from Yale College that bore the name Nathan Hale, but Howe believed it was only a cover for his real mission and he planned to expose this imposter.

Hale, captured earlier in the day presumably making his escape back to the American lines, was only twenty one years old, and his demeanor was more like a gentleman than a spy. The British captain who transported Hale to the headquarters, reported that he was awestruck that "such a fine fellow had fallen into their hands." But espionage was one of the most detested war crimes, and General Howe intended on issuing the most serious punishment.

With his hands tied behind his back, the young prisoner was ushered into Howe's headquarters, flanked by armed guards. He stood before the General, who would act as judge and jury for this quick trial. Howe immediately began the questioning and soon the accusations of spying. Hale continued to insist that he was a school teacher looking for employment. His response to each question was consistent, and his temperament was calm and collected and he stood tall and proud. He surely did not seem to possess the character of a spy, but then again neither did he appear to be a school teacher. The burn mark on his face also testified that this man was, or at least had been, a soldier.

Unknown to Hale, General Howe had evidence of his espionage, and he was about to expose him. Again he offered the young man the opportunity to confess, but again Hale stood tall proclaiming his search for a teaching job. Howe then produced the documents that were found inside the young man's shoe.

Hale was definitely an amateur in the espionage business and thought the documents were too well concealed to be found. But at the sight of these incriminating documents in the hands of the British, he and his mission were fully compromised. He was not only concerned about his fate, but that the important documents in Howe's hands would not make it back to General Washington.

The information found in Hale's shoe was extensive, and its disclosure could have been devastating to the British Army's plans to surround General Washington's Army, and force its surrender. However, unknown to Nathan Hale, a few days earlier General George Washington had abandoned his plans and pulled his Army off of Manhattan Island, the site of the possible skirmish. Although the information would be of little use now, the drawings of British fortifications, the location and strength of British elements, and the detailed maps pinpointing key British outposts, was exactly what Washington had tasked his young volunteer to obtain.

A soldier operating behind enemy lines in civilian attire was, by all accounts, a spy, and now that the documents had been discovered, there was no doubt left in Hale's mind that he would surely receive the punishment for espionage; death by hanging.

General Howe was standing and waiving the documents at Hale, demanding a full confession. Nathan began to speak, but not as was expected. A spy would have continued his ruse by denying the accusations, or pledging loyalty to the crown and offering to spy for the British. But Nathan's response was as a respectable officer who had been taken prisoner in combat, giving his name, rank and purpose of his mission. Everyone in the room was shocked at the behavior of this young man. He was clearly caught in the act of spying, but he responded as if he were a soldier on a mission.

Howe again accused him of treason against the King's Army. Hale again responded that he was Captain Nathan Hale, an officer in the Continental Army, and was on a military mission for General George Washington. The General was impressed by the courage and character of this young rebel, but Howe pronounced he was guilty of espionage and would be executed as such. Howe informed Hale that his execution would take place the following morning, Sunday, September 22, and until then, he would remain bound by the hands and feet and kept under guard. To the shock of everyone, Hale simply replied, "I regret that I had not been able to serve my country better."

In the short time since his capture, Captain Nathan Hale had made a strong impression on his captors. He displayed none of the characteristics of a typical spy, his conduct was that of a gentleman. While the duty of a spy was considered necessary in war, the common soldier believed only those of despicable character could perform such duties. Unlike the professional soldier, who wore a uniform openly declaring his loyalty and allegiance; the common spy was an actor and imposter with poor character who lived a solitary life of deception, befriended no one, and above all was the least to be trusted. But their remarkable young rebel prisoner had displayed none of these traits. He seemed to only display integrity, dignity and honor. Even one of the British soldiers appointed to guard Hale during his trial reported that

Nathan's patriotism, professional demeanor and dedication to duty had even touched General Howe.

Howe was indeed impressed by the strikingly handsome and brave young captain, but King George's orders were that all American rebels suspected of spying were to be immediately and quietly executed. Regardless of his impressions of Captain Hale, General Howe was an obedient and loyal subject to his King and was honor-bound to follow the will of the sovereign. Howe ordered Nathan to be placed in the custody of Provost Marshall Cunningham until time for the execution.

As the guards grabbed him by the arms and started to escort him out of the headquarters, Nathan, addressing the General, made two requests. First, that a chaplain be present at his execution, and second, that a Bible be provided for him to read while he awaited the hanging. The General promptly denied both requests as he motioned for the guards to take Nathan away. He was immediately taken to the estate's greenhouse, where his hands and feet were securely tied, and he was placed under the watchful eyes of two armed sentries.

For the first time since his capture, Nathan was alone. Unless God decided to miraculously intervene, he knew he had but a few short hours left in his young life. Without a Bible to comfort him, Nathan spent the last night of his life praying and reciting many of the verses he had memorized.

It was not uncommon for a man sentenced to death, regardless of how sinful he was, to suddenly decide he needed the comfort of religion. But this was not the case for Nathan Hale. Prayer and devotion had been a daily activity for him since early childhood, and he was simply carrying out his normal routine.

CONNECTICUT SCHOOL TEACHER

Nathan Hale was born on June 6, 1755 in Coventry, Connecticut. He was the sixth of ten children born to Richard and
Elizabeth Strong Hale, who lived on a farm in Coventry. His
parents were staunch puritans who raised Nathan with a great
respect for prayer and devotion, a dedication to hard work, and
an appreciation for education. At the young age of fourteen,
Nathan and his brother Enoch left home to attend college at
Yale. Biblical studies were mandatory at Yale, and students were
required to attended services each morning at the school's
chapel. Nathan, wanting a time of private devotion, arose at four
thirty every morning to pray before attending chapel services.

While most of his Yale classmates were studying to enter the
ministry, Nathan set his sights on teaching. Upon graduating, at
the age of eighteen, Nathan accepted his first teaching position
at a small school in Moodus, Connecticut, a country town just
thirty miles south of his hometown of Coventry. After a short
tenure at the Moodus school, Nathan was given the opportunity
to interview for a more prestigious position in New London.
The Union School in New London was seeking a new schoolmaster and, although Nathan was considered too young for such
a prestigious position, he came highly recommended, so the
school founders agreed to at least give him the honor of an interview.

New London was a bustling seaport city, much larger and
more socially active than the laid back country town of Moodus.
The Union School could accommodate up to forty students,
which made it much larger than most schools in colonial
America. Nathan was excited by the thought of living in a busy
and vibrant town. He was equally excited about the prospect of

attaining such a prestigious position as schoolmaster of the Union School.

Despite his youth and limited experience, the town leaders were impressed with Nathan's intelligence, personality, dedication to God and his high moral standards. They saw potential in this young man, and considering the recommendations he received from some of Connecticut's most respected leaders, they offered him a position as temporary schoolmaster.

At nineteen years old, Nathan was only a couple years older than some of his students. This would have normally caused concern by parents and town leaders, but Nathan's values and strong moral character so impressed the families that they eagerly embraced their young new schoolmaster. As it was expected in all classrooms of that time, Nathan not only taught the Bible but he incorporated theology into his teaching of academics. As one who regularly studied the scriptures, Nathan knew, as the book of Proverbs taught, that "The fear of the Lord is the beginning of knowledge," so he began every school day by leading his class in prayer. Nathan's teaching had a long lasting affect on his students, including one of his older students, Nathanial Green. Green, who would later serve as one of George Washington's most trusted Colonels, said that he was greatly influenced by Nathan's "fine moral character."

All of Nathan's regular students were boys, as it was the standard in colonial America that only the males attended school. But he believed the young ladies of New London should also have the opportunity to attend classes, so he organized a special school, exclusively for young ladies, during the summer. Since he still conducted classes for the males, his all girl school ran from five to seven o'clock in the morning. The fact that several of the town's young ladies were eager enough to attend at such an early hour may have been a testament to their thirst for knowledge, but it could also have been due in part to the teacher's striking good looks.

Nathan Hale exceeded all the expectations of the school founders and, later that year, was offered a permanent position as the town's schoolmaster. Nathan felt at home in New London. He enjoyed the job and the excitement of life in a large city but, more importantly, he loved the students. Nathan eagerly accepted their offer.

Nathan enjoyed life in New London, and was one of the town's most respected citizens. He was also one of New London's most eligible and desirable bachelors. Admired by many of the young ladies, it was not long before rumors of a budding relationship with an attractive young lady began to circulate. Everything was going well for Nathan, and he believed he had finally found his life's calling. But while Nathan's future seemed safe and secure, the rumors of rebellion against England were beginning to brew. Soon Nathan would hear another call; one that would lead him away from his home, his family and friends, to whom he would never return. It was a compelling call to patriotic duty.

CAPTAIN JOHN MONTRESOR

Other than the armed soldiers Provost Marshall Cunningham positioned outside the door of the greenhouse, Nathan was alone, as the sun set for the last time of his short life. His situation was somewhat similar to that of the Apostle Paul, who had been cast into prison for preaching a message that freed men from the oppression of sin. Nathan was imprisoned because of a mission to help free men from tyranny. One difference was that Paul had been allowed to write letters during his time in prison. Nathan, however, was not afforded the privilege of paper and quill. But like Paul, Nathan had the gospel story stored away in his memory and, even without a Bible, he could recite numerous passages of scripture. So Nathan Hale waited through the night, his hands and ankles shackled, quoting scripture and praying.

As the sun broke the horizon the next morning, Nathan expected the guards to arrive at any moment to take him to the gallows. General Howe's orders had been that he was to be executed in the morning but, when the door opened, Nathan was greeted by a British officer who introduced himself as Captain John Montresor, General Howe's Chief Engineer. Montresor told Nathan that he was to be relocated and interviewed while preparations were made for the execution. The guards escorted Nathan to Montresor's tent, which was only a short distance from where a detail was preparing the site for his hanging.

Montresor had seen the confiscated documents and, as an engineer, he was impressed by the detail. Studying the documents, he realized the author was not only well educated but had an understanding of cartography and engineering practices. Howe wanted to know more about the documents and how the information was obtained, so he asked Montresor to interrogate Nathan before the execution. Montresor thought the interview would be better conducted in a more comfortable environment, so he requested that Nathan be brought to his quarters.

While Nathan and Montresor talked, Cunningham continued preparations for the execution. For some unknown reason, probably due to a night of hard drinking, Cunningham was behind schedule. He located an apple tree in a nearby orchard, found a sturdy limb, and called for a length of rope and a wooden ladder to be brought to the site. He then ordered Bill Richmond, a thirteen year-old former slave, to secure the rope to the tree and fasten a noose.

As the hangmen worked a short distance away, Montresor and Nathan's conversation quickly moved from the technical aspects of the documents, to Nathan's personal life. Montresor noted that the young American captain possessed none of the qualities associated with a spy. He found Nathan to be an honest gentleman, full of love and compassion, with an obvious dedication to God and his country. Montresor recognized that Nathan was out of place in the world of espionage, and was impressed with the poise, self respect and dignity he displayed during their time together. Unlike Cunningham, who was a wretched man who enjoyed the duty of executioner, Montresor was a gentleman, and treated Nathan with professional courtesy and respect. The more they talked, the more compassionate Montresor became towards Nathan's fate. Although they were enemies in war, Montresor intended to bring some comfort in the final hours of this young man's life. Nathan confessed that he had succumbed to the inevitable, but had committed the out-come into the hands of God. Throughout the morning, Nathan remained poised and spoke with dignity, not what one would expect of someone about to face a cruel death.

Learning that it was Nathan's daily habit to pray, Montresor allowed him time to pray for his family and friends who would be left to grieve his death, and the soldiers that would carry on the fight for liberty. Hale was unsure how his many friends and family would ever learn of his fate. He did not want his legacy to be one of a failed spy, but as a soldier who gave his life in the line of duty. He realized that if history would have any account of him at all, the story told would be determined by his captors.

FROM TEACHER TO SOLDIER

In March of 1775 , following the British attacks on American colonists at Lexington and Concord, a town meeting was called at the Miner's Tavern in New London. The townspeople were angry, and there were cries for armed rebellion. The British Army had killed forty-nine colonists. The Massachusetts minutemen responded with vengeance, and sent the British into a full retreat back to Boston. The talk of rebellion was no longer a rumor, and the winds of war were beginning to blow. The meeting was called to determine how New London would respond to the British aggression. Judge Richard Law presided and, once he was able to get order, he recognized Captain William Coit, the commander of the New London volunteers, to address the situation. Coit announced that a Continental Army was being organized near Boston and suggested that it was time for his militia to join them. After a lengthy and passionate discussion, it was decided that Captain Coit should muster his volunteers and plan to depart for Boston as soon as possible. Coit announced that he and his citizen soldiers were ready to march, and they would depart the following morning.

When Coit sat down, Nathan stood and asked to be recognized. As always, Nathan spoke eloquently with great passion and conviction. As most of the people of New London, Nathan believed it was time to take up arms. The young schoolmaster announced that he intended to join Coit's volunteers, and Nathan urged other men to do the same saying, "Let us march immediately and never lay down our arms until we obtain our independence." Soon, the inspired crowd dismissed and returned to their homes. Some prepared their personal and business affairs so they could join Coit in the fight for independence. Nathan returned home where he undoubtedly spent the remainder of the evening praying for God's divine guidance.

As Coit's volunteers marched off toward Boston, Nathan addressed his students. It was a very difficult and emotional time for Nathan, as his students were very close to his heart, and he had to inform them of his decision to join the army and leave New London. The students were distraught at losing their teacher, so their schoolmaster made time to speak with each one individually. After consulting them, he called the class together and, holding hands, they knelt down and prayed.

While Nathan had felt the call to patriotic duty, he also had a responsibility to the school, so instead of hurrying off to join with Coit's militia, Nathan applied for a commission in the regular army. This would give him time to hand over his duties as schoolmaster and prepare for military service. A short time later, he received a commission as an officer in the Connecticut Army, said farewell to his students, and joined the Seventh Regiment under the command of Colonel Charles Webb.

Nathan remained in Connecticut with the regiment while they organized and trained. In late June, word arrived that an element of American volunteers, mostly Massachusetts men, had engaged the British on the outskirts of Boston in an area known as Bunker Hill. Although the Americans put up a spirited and brave fight, the British eventually won the day and now occupied the town of Boston. In September, Nathan was promoted to Captain and assigned as second in command of the Third Company under Major Jonathon Lattimor. General

George Washington of Virginia had been chosen by Congress as Commander in Chief of the Continental Army, and he called upon the legislatures of the colonies to send troops and supplies to Cambridge, where he was preparing a siege on Boston. Shortly thereafter, Hale's regiment received orders and promptly marched off to Cambridge.

Life in camp was significantly different than what Nathan was accustomed to in New London. Sickness and disease were common, as men lived in close quarters under less than desirable, and sometimes deplorable conditions. As an officer, Nathan faced other challenges, such as the drinking and unruliness of idle men. One night, while patrolling the camp, Nathan happened upon a group of rambunctious and obviously intoxicated soldiers playing cards. Gambling and drinking were strictly forbidden, and Nathan gave them a stern lecture on the responsibility of maintaining order in the camp. The men so highly respected their captain that they willingly surrendered their playing cards, and never uttered an ill word of the incident.

Regardless of how difficult the situation or lamentable the conditions, Nathan held fast to his faith. As men fell ill to disease and deprivation, common among the American camps, Nathan tended his men with great care and compassion. Although he was younger than most of the men in his unit, his strong character and attention to their well being, quickly earned their respect and loyalty. Nathan was often seen kneeling beside men stricken with illness, "with a Bible in one hand, the hand of an ill soldier in the other, praying aloud for his recovery."

THE RANGERS

Inside Montresor's tent, Nathan patiently awaited his final walk. Montresor knew that Nathan's time was drawing short, and asked if there was anything he could do. Nathan requested some writing material so he could write a couple of letters.

Montresor knew Cunningham strictly prohibited condemned prisoners, especially spies, to send letters before their execution. But Montresor secretly obtained paper, quill and an ink and brought them to the tent. While Montresor kept watch, Nathan wrote two letters; one to his brother Enoch and the second to his current commander, Colonel Knowlton.

Nathan had frequently corresponded with his family, especially his brother, but since volunteering with the Knowlton Rangers, an elite covert unit that took on the most risky missions, Nathan wrote very little. After being selected by the unit's commander, Colonel Thomas Knowlton, to serve as one of his intelligence gathering officers, Nathan did not share details of his service, since most of his missions were highly secretive. No one, other than Colonel Knowlton, a few of his fellow Rangers, and General Washington, knew that he had volunteered for the mission for which he was about to die. It was quite possible that no one on the American side would ever know what happened to him, and he did not want to leave this world without saying goodbye.

Several weeks before his capture, Nathan volunteered for this mission, which he was told was critical to the cause of liberty. With the British occupying Long Island, Washington was desperate to know the strength of the British Army as well as the location and design of their defensive fortifications. Washington was in a very dire situation. He was heavily outnumbered, flanked on at least three sides by British forces, and at risk of being cut off by British ships patrolling the East and Hudson Rivers.

Washington needed intelligence information on the British strengths and strategic plans, so he approached Colonel Knowlton with a request to send one of his Rangers into New York, undercover, to obtain the needed information. Knowlton's Rangers were quickly becoming a legend among the Continental Army, and they were the most likely to pull off such a dangerous mission. Knowlton had recruited one hundred fifty of the best soldiers in the American Army to join his elite unit. Upon receiving an invitation, Nathan enthusiastically volunteered for the Rangers, and Knowlton was soon impressed by Nathan's leadership, loyalty and especially his knowledge of science and engineering.

Although Nathan was a fit man for Washington's undercover mission, he was not Knowlton's first choice. One of Nathan's cousins, also a Ranger, was given the first opportunity, but the young man promptly refused, stating that spying was not becoming of a soldier and that "death wasn't a possibility; but a certainty, if one was caught in civilian clothes behind enemy lines."

Following what he believed was only the first of several refusals yet to come, Knowlton called a meeting. Knowing that Nathan was suffering with a severe case of influenza, Knowlton did not invite him. Somehow, word reached Nathan of the meeting and, although he was barely able to stand, he stumbled to the blockhouse just in time to hear Knowlton's request. To the astonishment of everyone in the room, Nathan, who was extremely pale and sweating profusely from fever, stepped forward and said, "I will undertake it, sir." Their surprise was not as much due to his illness, but rather that an honest, honorable and well respected officer would volunteer for a suicide mission.

Immediately, several of his fellow Rangers began trying to discourage Nathan from accepting this risky and potentially suicidal duty. Several surrounded him and tried to appeal to his sense of responsibility. They spoke of his home, his family and the promising future that he was risking. But Nathan had made his decision and explained, "I am fully sensible of the consequences...but for a year I have been attached to the Army and have not rendered any material service while receiving compensation for which I make no return." Unwilling to discuss the matter any further, Nathan left the meeting and returned to his quarters.

Captain William Hull was quite possibly Nathan's closest friend. They had known each other at Yale, and their relationship grew when they were assigned to the same regiment under the command of Colonel Webb. They trained together at New London and served side by side in Cambridge.

Hull, hearing of Nathan's decision, was waiting in his tent when he returned from the meeting. Nathan explained Washington's request and asked Hull his opinion. Hull immediately tried to dissuade him, arguing that spying was not in Nathan's character and, quite frankly, he was incapable of acting the part. He told Nathan that although the business of a spy was a necessary duty; it was one that could not be forced upon a soldier. He advised Nathan that he could easily back out without any reflection upon himself as an officer. Nathan was still committed and as their discussion continued, Hull reminded Nathan that "few respect the character of a spy," and it was not considered an honorable service. Nathan responded, "I wish to be useful, and every kind of service, necessary to the public good, becomes honorable by being necessary." In one last attempt to change his friend's mind, Hull asked him to reflect upon his love for his country and the friends that he would surely leave behind. This argument seemed to have touched Nathan, as he paused momentarily in deep thought. But after a few moments of silent reflection, Nathan grabbed Hull's hand and said, "I will reflect, and do nothing but what duty demands."

In the opinion of those who knew Nathan, he was the least likely of the Rangers to accept such a calling, and the least likely soldier to succeed. He was not the type of man one would expect in the role of a spy. He was a devout Christian who was not ashamed of his faith. Not only was he regularly seen praying for his men and their beloved cause, but he prayed without hesitation for anyone in need. On one occasion, when a fellow soldier was mortally wounded, Nathan knelt beside him in the marsh and prayed as the young soldier passed on into eternity. When his personal servant fell ill during their encampment at Cambridge, Nathan knelt beside his bed for several days and nights praying for his recovery. Another of Nathan's personal servants, Asher Wright, said that Nathan was one of the most devout men that he had ever known, and referred to him as the "praying man."

The Death March

Nathan finished writing the letters to his brother and Colonel Knowlton and was soon summoned from the tent. It was a beautiful fall morning in the countryside of Manhattan Island. The sun shone brightly, birds sang and a small band of townspeople began to assemble along the small sloping ridge where a lone rope hung from the limb of an apple tree. The execution party was assembled and ready, some even eager, to perform their macabre duty. Outside the tent, Cunningham and several armed men waited to escort Nathan to the gallows. With both letters securely clutched in his hand, Nathan began his death march. Cunningham led the execution party as they walked up the narrow path. Nathan was surrounded by guards, whose duty it was to prevent him from running. But that was not an option for Nathan; he was an officer and a patriot, and running would be a cowardly act unfitting of a man of his character. Although he was not part of the execution detail, Montresor followed a few paces behind.

British executions were typically held privately as to not expose the public to the horrors and pain of death by hanging. Executions were mostly conducted around midnight, and citizens were strictly forbidden to watch. Residents in the area were usually ordered to stay indoors with their windows and shutters closed. A chaplain was normally at the scene to say a prayer for the soul of the convicted before their death. As soon as death was confirmed, the bodies were quickly removed, and immediately buried at or near the site of their execution. By daybreak, all evidence of the execution would be removed.

Nathan Hale would not be afforded this amount of respect. Cunningham allowed those who lived in the area to witness the hanging of the American spy. Men and women stood along each side of the trail as the young handsome man, hands bound behind his back, quietly passed by. Some may have heckled Nathan for being a rebel and a spy, but most just stood quietly and watched. Fully aware that he was the main attraction in this horrifying parade, Nathan marched on with the poise and dignity of a soldier. He walked erect with his head held high and his eyes always looking forward. He appeared more like an officer marching with his troops, than a man who was about to face death. As Nathan and his escorts passed by, the onlookers were encouraged to file in behind and follow.

On top of the hill, in the midst of an apple orchard, several soldiers were gathered around a tree. A single rope with a noose tied at the end swung lightly in the breeze. A ladder was positioned under the rope and, as Nathan made his final few steps toward the ladder, the execution party took their places. Although there were several soldiers and officers standing around the tree, one was obviously missing; a chaplain. It was clear that, although his death would be witnessed by many, there would be no ceremony, no words of comfort and no prayer for his soon departing soul.

Cunningham approached Nathan and asked if he had "any last dying speech and confession." Nathan handed Cunningham the two letters and asked if he would kindly send them. Cunningham refused, saying, "The rebels should never know that they had a man who could die with such firmness." He took the letters from Nathan, and they were never sent nor seen again. Nathan stated that he was an officer in the Continental Army and requested execution by a firing squad, which Cunningham promptly refused. Besides the fact that a firing squad was a more humane method of execution, it was also a more honorable method used for soldiers. Hanging was for criminals, deserters and spies, and Cunningham intended for Nathan to leave this world at the end of a rope. Nathan showed no expression of dread or disappointment, he just bravely stepped forward and climbed the ladder.

The rope was placed around Nathan's neck and, immediately, several of the young ladies who had been brought to witness the hanging, began to cry. Cunningham cursed the crowd, and warned the onlookers that if they did not remain quiet they may find themselves also on the gallows.

A soldier tightened the rope around Nathan's neck, then climbed down the ladder as the rest of the execution party stepped away. The crowd fell quiet as the final seconds ticked away in the young life of Nathan Hale. He stood alone on the ladder, with the rope around his neck with his head held skyward as if he were looking into heaven. The silence was broken as Nathan, still looking upward, began to speak. Cunningham expected to hear a final plea for mercy or a confession of his espionage, but his hopes were quickly dashed as Nathan exclaimed, "You are shedding the blood of the innocent. If I had ten thousand lives, I would lay them all down, if called to do it, in defense of my injured, bleeding country."

Hearing those words of defiance, Cunningham shouted, "Swing the rebel off!" and the ladder was kicked out from under Nathan. He fell a short distance, then his body jerked as the slack in the rope ran out. The force, created by his falling body being snatched to a stop, caused the rope to tighten around his neck. The more fortunate victims of hanging had their necks broken as their vertebrae were crushed by the force of the rope suddenly contracting at the end of their fall. This was more common among large and heavier men, but Nathan was in excellent physical condition, and it was more likely that death came with more pain and agony as the rope cut off his airflow and he slowly suffocated.

NEVER TO RETURN

Off the coast of Long Island, the *Shuyler,* an armed American sloop, patrolled the shoreline looking for a signal, but none was seen. Seven days earlier under the cover of darkness, the ship's captain, Charles Pond, watched as Captain Nathan Hale, dressed in brown civilian clothes wearing a Dutch style broad brimmed hat, stepped off the ship. Just before he departed, the Captain noticed Hale turn to Sergeant Steven Hempstead, who had accompanied him since they left the American camp. Hale handed Sergeant Hempstead his watch as they said goodbye. Captain Hale saluted the sergeant and disappeared into the trees.

Captain Pond was to rendezvous with Nathan along this same point, but there was no signal from the shore. The ship waited until it was certain that Nathan did not make it to the pickup point, then returned to its homeport of Norwalk, Connecticut. Word was sent to General George Washington that the officer sent into New York did not return, and his status was uncertain. Washington did not have to notify Knowlton, as he had been killed in action the day Nathan had departed for New York.

A few days later, a British officer appeared at the American lines bearing a white flag of truce. The officer was a Captain by the name of Montresor, bearing a letter from General Howe for General Washington. The letter was given to an American officer, who forwarded it on to Washington, and Montresor awaited the reply. Montresor stated that he had additional information about an American officer by the name of Nathan Hale, who had been executed as a spy in New York. Montresor gave a full account of Nathan, and told how he had befriended him before the execution. He told how Hale maintained his loyalty and dedication to the American cause even to the final moments of his death. He told them that Cunningham had left Nathan's body hanging on the tree for three days before it was cut down and buried at the site of the execution. He then told them of the final words of Captain Nathan Hale. They were words of an officer loyal to his cause and, though history would paraphrase them as, "I only regret that I have but one life to lose for my country," they were the final and lasting sentiments of a Christian, a patriot, a solder and, more importantly, a man of prayer, who's words would inspire generations of Americans.

REFERENCES

McCullough, David G. *1776: Excerpts from the Acclaimed History, with Letters, Maps, and Seminal Artwork.* New York: Simon & Schuster, 2007. Print.

Phelps, M. William. *Nathan Hale: the Life and Death of America's First Spy.* New York: Thomas Dunne, 2008. Print.

Souter, Gerry. *The Founding Fathers, The Shaping of America.* London: Sevenoaks, 2009. Print.

Ortner, Mary J. "Captain Nathan Hale (1755-1776) - Sons of the American Revolution, Connecticut." *Connecticut Society of the Sons of the American Revolution - CTSSAR.* Web. 17 Apr. 2011. <http://www.connecticutsar.org/patriots/hale_nathan_2.htm>.

FastPencil
http://www.fastpencil.com